FINDING GOD IN YOUR HOUSE:

The best of Bringing Religion Home

By James Breig

THE THOMAS MORE PRESS
Chicago, Illinois

27299942

ISBN 0-88347-266-X

TABLE OF CONTENTS

To my wife Mary
(this time, for her courage)
and to my children,
Jim, Matt and Carrie
(always for their love)

INTRODUCTION

THE stories you're about to read first appeared in a monthly newsletter called Bringing Religion Home, published by Claretian Publications of Chicago. Each word of the newsletter's title has something important to say about these stories:

*Bringing: Some people have questioned the use of this word. They prefer "finding" or "developing" or "nurturing." After all, they argue, religion isn't something you bring home from the store like a quart of milk. It's something which should be there already or something which is hidden but can be brought to the surface. That criticism misses the meaning of an expression we use all the time when a very significant idea reaches our minds; when that happens, we say, "That point was brought home to me." It's in that sense that these stories try to bring religion home.

*Religion: This word is shorthand for a lot of things: morality, spirituality, prayer, the love of God and such family treasures as memories and mirth—in other words, all the components of family life which take seriously the relationship we have with our Creator.

*Home: There are all kinds of these: single-parent households, step-families, racially or religiously mixed marriages, single persons who keep in touch with other family members living far away, elderly people in nursing homes. We all have homes, even the homeless who live on the streets, because a home is where we find those who love us. And that can be anywhere.

Bringing Religion Home . . . or Nurturing Spirituality In Your Families . . . or Developing A Love For Jesus Among Your Children—whatever the title over them, these stories are about how you and your family can bring religion home and preserve it there.

James Breig

FOREWORD:

The first spring of Robin and Marian

WHEN fall comes and a chill is in the morning air and everyone's thinking of what sort of winter it will be, I wonder where Robin and Marian are. I especially worry about their three offspring. Because I witnessed their births and earliest days, that trio has stayed in my memory and I sometimes scan the skies, imagining that they are winging overhead.

Robin, Marian and their youngsters are all birds. They came into our family's lives one spring when a robin began building her nest in our morning newspaper. Each day when I would fetch the paper from the mail slot in our front door, I'd find shreds of grass all over it.

Frustrated at my daily destruction of her work, the robin began trying to build her home on a decorative pillar on our porch, an impossible feat since the space was only about an inch square.

After two weeks of this, I called the Audubon Society. The woman there laughed at my predicament but warned me about what might happen: "They're very persistent. If you keep moving the nest from the newspaper, some morning you're going to find that she's laid her eggs anyway. Try to give her an alternative."

So Mr. Handyman (a nickname I earned from all my efforts around the house—like knowing exactly how far to turn up the volume on the TV set) fetched a ladder, hammer, nails and a bit of plasterboard from the basement. To the small pillar I attached an outcrop, an ideal place for a robin to build a nest.

On a rainy weekend, she went to work. She and her husband (naturally I named him Robin, so she had to be Marian) flew back and forth, delivering bits of grass to their new perch. As they arrived, she would squish them down and spread out her wings, forming a bowl from the shapeless material. Feathering her nest is the term, I guess; for that's what she did.

I watched from our front window, fascinated by how the two worked together. The encyclopedia informed me that both male and female would work together on the nest building, and they did. It was amazing to see how quickly the duo produced a sturdy, solid cup for the eggs to come.

During the next several days, our whole family took turns watching from the front window and, occasionally, taking a peek into the nest through the window at the top of our front door. Those peeks were limited, though, because they invariably frightened Marian, who sat faithfully on the nest.

Watching over her was Robin. When an interloping bird would invade their territory, he would swoop down from nearby branches and chase off the visitor.

One warm Friday afternoon, I climbed the ladder in our vestibule to look inside the nest and saw three blue eggs. If naming the parents Robin and Marian wasn't corny enough, I now named the three babies Larry, Doug and Admiral. The Birds— get it? (Most people understand Larry and Admiral, but I have to explain that Doug Bird was a rather undistinguished major-league pitcher.)

About a week later, those eggs turned into three ugly little offspring, each with a sizable yellow beak and very few feathers.

Finding God in Your House

Everyone took turns watching Robin and Marian feed and care for their babies. When the Mrs. was off eating, hubby stayed on the nest, looking like all human fathers when left in charge—slightly annoyed, but obviously proud.

Within a few weeks, the homely brood became too large for the nest and two of them disappeared. One stayed behind, peeping for his family, looking very lonely and afraid. It must have been Doug. Then, late one evening, a check of the nest revealed that it was empty.

I waited a few more days and then removed the nest. I was surprised by how heavy and substantial it was, as if it had been woven. Our 9-year-old took it to school for show-and-tell, and our two teenagers pronounced the entire affair boring, but my wife, Mary, and I felt something a little more keen.

"This is silly," Mary said to me shortly after the last one had flown the coop, "but I'm worried about them. Where are they?"

I shrugged, and we held each other. We were both thinking about our own three offspring and how soon they would be gone.

Every summer I look at robins a little differently and try to guess which ones might be "ours." And now I wonder where they are, if they're all right, and if they'll be back some spring.

CHAPTER 1

Parents in action and reaction

There's nothing like children to create an immortal soul

I wish Mary and I had had more children.

If there's too narrow a gap between our sons (eleven months), there is too large a hiatus between them and our daughter (eight years) and between her birth and now (ten years).

We could have fit two or three more kids in there.

When I start talking about this, Mary eyes me suspiciously and begins backing away. A realist, she remembers both the good times and the bad times: the babies with birthday-cake mustaches who became the teenagers with cigarette breath. A dreamer, I screen out the realities of raising children and nostalgically long for another boy to play catch with, another girl to tickle, or even twins to do both with.

So my reasons are, initially, very selfish. I want more children because of the happiness and fun they would have given me. Lately, however, I've been thinking of another reason we should have had more children, a reason I'll bet most parents don't consider. It has nothing to do with building a family or bringing joy into a home. It has to do with metaphysics.

When parents conceive a child, they and God create something that did not exist a moment before: an immortal soul. That person—male or female, handicapped or perfect, black or white or brown—will live forever.

James Breig

That's a part of childbearing that parents don't think about often enough. We think of our babies turning into toddlers and going off to first grade and graduating from high school and getting a job. Time stretches before them, filled with opportunity and hope and dreams. Parents imagine that future only as far as adulthood for their children, with some vague notion of their living on after our deaths. But we should think of them existing eternally. Because they will.

That's why parenting is such a blessing and a burden, such a joy and a challenge, such a calling and an obligation. We shouldn't have children just to turn them into A students or top engineers or successful accountants or the president of the country. All that, in the end, is meaningless when you consider that their life span on earth is so brief compared to their eternal happiness after they die.

Imagine, therefore, what conceiving a child is: giving the gift of eternal life and, hopefully, eternal joy to someone you don't even know. As a parent, I know the happiness I get out of giving gifts to my children. Seeing their faces light up over something they've wanted or when I treat them to a surprise brings immeasurable joy to my life. What unlimited feelings of happiness will I have if I see my children in heaven (or vice versa)?

I mentioned these thoughts to a new mother the other day and asked if she had ever considered them. She had.

"They scare me sometimes," she said. "What if I mess up with my son? What if we don't raise him right? What if I can't pass our faith on to him?"

I wish Mary and I had had more children so that more people would have the chance to know eternal bliss. Do you ever think of that when you look at your children or when you decide how many to have? I know there are all sorts of factors to consider when making the choice to have another child, but I wonder if we include the most important factor in the mix when we do our deciding.

How to help your grown-up kids remain Catholic

When my sons, Jimmy and Matt, were in grade school, I felt the pressure of introducing them to God and religion. What a burden, I thought; their ideas of the most important topics in the universe depend on me. Surely nothing is more difficult than that.

Then my sons got to high school and I felt the pressure of answering their questions about evolution, abortion, the seeming absence of God in their lives at times, world starvation, and why they should get out of bed to go to Mass. Now *that's* a burden, I thought; their emerging individuality depends on me to offer some course correction and guidance. Definitely, nothing is more difficult than that.

Now my sons are in college and I've discovered a fact that should confound physicists: the heaviest pressure is felt when there's no burden at all. The exciting era of introducing my sons to God has passed; the energetic age of answering their questions and meeting their challenges is gone. We have arrived at a new epoch, and it is a time of silence when boys become men and children establish a new relationship with their parents. They don't come to Dad seeking advice anymore.

So what's a mom or dad to do when kids are no longer kids but you still want to help them know, love and serve God? That's what I've been asking myself, my wife and my sons lately; and

I've come up with some strategies that allow children their freedom while also keeping rights for parents. After all, no matter how old they get, they are still "the kids." Here are my strategies for keeping kids Catholic when they become adults:

1. Prayer: the first idea is the most obvious. It's the age-old weapon parents have that children cannot subvert. In moments of meditation at Mass, in bedtime prayers, at small-group prayer sessions and during other times of prayer, mothers and fathers can link their children to God.

If it sometimes seems that the young ones are no longer listening, you're guaranteed that God is. Speak to God about how you feel and what you think your children need; ask God to stay in their lives even if they try to withdraw and seek guidance on how you should behave so that you don't smother or drive your children away when you're trying to help.

2. Acceptance: parents have to face the fact that children get out on their own socially, politically, and religiously as they grow. In other words, I have to accept that my sons are now adults and deserve to be treated as such. That means breaking a twenty-year-old habit, and that's not easy.

It also means developing a virtue parents sometimes have trouble with: humility. It means admitting that you don't have all the answers to religious faith; it means recognizing that just because your children practice their faith differently from you doesn't mean they aren't practicing it (they could even be practicing it better than you); it means realizing that sometimes you can learn from your children; it means being able to shut up when you most want to shout out.

3. Letting go: this is the really tough one for most parents. After twenty years or so of being responsible for your children,

Finding God in Your House

it's difficult to cut the apron strings and let go of their hands. But that's what has to happen if they are to become mature persons, which, after all, is one of the goals you set when you decided to have children.

Little by little, my sons have been going out on their own; picking friends, selecting their own reading, choosing which college courses to take, deciding which Mass to attend.

"You can't force us anymore," Jimmy, 19, said to me. "We have to decide now."

Part of letting go is living with their bad decisions. For many parents, this means suffering through their children's apostasy. More and more sociologists are finding the same thing: young adults wander from their faith for a few years while they test the secular waters. Then most of them come back home. What grays Daddy's hair is both the interim period and the realization that his sons could be among the portion who don't come home.

"We just have to hope our lessons when they were young were enough," my wife said. "Think of what we did: we sent them to Catholic school, we prayed with them, we gave them religious books and magazines to read, we talked about God and prayer. We have to rely on what we did when they were little and hope they remember it."

4. Tricks: okay, I'll pray, accept and let go. But I'm not above a little subversion. I have developed some nefarious ways to try to make sure my sons continue to take religion seriously. For example, I bring home religious newspapers and publications and leave them where my sons might pick them up. I place them near the piles of college textbooks that can be found here and there in our house; I leave them on bedroom floors, a pop-

15

ular place for reading matter to congregate; I've even slipped them onto bathroom counters for moments when they've forgotten to bring in a sports magazine.

And it works. I find the books opened on night stands. The magazines pop up in different locations with the pages crinkled. The topics contained in the reading materials come up in conversations.

At dinner one night, I remarked that maybe my sons could use some fresh religious education. Matt, 18, responded with "We read those books you bring home, you know."

Here are some other tricky ways to keep religion alive:

• Drop hints about parish activities they could participate in, for example, as volunteers for some event or as lay ministers.

• Search out parishes in your areas that offer Masses for young adults or that have reputations for attracting that age group; then let your children know about them.

• When religious and spiritual topics come up on a TV show or in the newspaper, bring them up as part of the family conversation. Your kids may deny it, but they are interested in what you have to say about such matters.

5. Example: finally, don't forget the method that probably got your kids to remain Catholic in the first place. It wasn't religious education; it was your example. I could recount a thousand stories about how my parents were good examples of living, praying, thinking and being. If my kids can say the same about me—along with tales of my foibles—then I've got a leg up on keeping them Catholic.

My example cannot stop just because they're older. In the end, the simple rule of teaching little ones about faith applies equally when the little ones grow tall: I have to go on living my faith if I expect my children to live theirs.

(Thanks to *Our Sunday Visitor* for permission to reprint this article.)

A little child shall lead them

It happened on a summer Saturday. Number one son was on his way out to a baseball game. Number two son wanted to exit to play with friends. Daughter was looking forward to a birthday party she had been invited to. I had some writing to finish. My wife, after a week of working extra hours because of staff shake-ups at her office, faced chores that hadn't been completed during the past seven days.

That's when the pizza hit the window.

Someone had somehow smeared a glump of pizza on the large window that divides our dining room from the kitchen. The only explanation: it had been thrown.

"Who did it?" asked my wife.

The answer came three times: "Not me." (I don't like pizza; so I was clean.)

"No one is leaving this house until I know who did it," their mother declared.

Uh-oh, I said to myself. She just backed herself into a corner. Parents do it all the time. We announce that X is dependent on Y when we know—in our rational moments—that we have no intention of keeping the dependency in force. The trouble is, sometimes moms and dads don't act rationally.

I remember once when I informed my sons that if the kitchen light was left on one more time they would not be allowed out of the house. Ever.

That time, my wife had to step in and act as the Great Compromiser when my older son left the light on and was due to leave the house for some important event at school.

Now, with the pizza smear, she had got herself into the same sort of "I wish I could bend, but I can't" situation.

Stubbornly, she refused to alter her conditions. Stubbornly, whoever threw the pizza refused to admit his or her guilt. To do so now would add lying to the list of crimes.

Meanwhile, the exit times ticked closer.

Finally, it was the 7-year-old girl who displayed the most intelligence—and self-sacrifice.

"I'll clean it up," Carrie said. "I didn't do it, but I'll clean it up so we can go."

Her willingness to scrub the window in her party dress inspired me to get the rag and cleanser and remove the tomato-and-cheese stain.

Everyone went their way, and peace was restored.

A little child shall lead them—by showing how selflessness works a lot better than stubbornness.

In giving, you receive

My daughter Carrie, 7, is loony for balloons, especially if they are helium ballons. If she can get her hands on a balloon, she's happy for hours—or at least until the helium dissipates.

God often uses the things people love to teach them lessons, and he used two recently to make a point (but not a sharp one!) to Carrie.

Friends came over for an evening of chat and brought with them two helium balloons, one pink and one purple. They

18

handed them both to Carrie but made it clear that she was to give one to another girl who would be arriving soon with her parents.

"I'll give Christie the purple one," Carrie informed me.

It was obvious she wanted the pink one and thought the purple one was ugly.

"The polite thing," I said, "would be to let Christie choose since she's a guest."

Carrie mulled it over and, as usual, recognized my wisdom.

When Christie arrived, Carrie held out the two prizes and said, "Which do you want?"

Without hesitation, Christie selected the purple one.

That night Carrie learned a lesson in hospitality and was instantly rewarded. I like it when God works like that.

When I was your age . . .

I'm a great believer in the power of stories. All kinds of stories. The Bible is stories. Great literature is stories. More people are moved by a dramatic tale than by a political speech. Who was it who said something like, "Let me control a nation's stories, and you can have its army"?

It works in families, too. Children often moan and make faces when parents begin talking about their childhood, but I believe that kids listen and remember. I remember my father's story of his boyhood when he was caught in a narrow alleyway unable to outrun an oncoming (and horse-drawn) fire truck. A leap onto a fire escape saved his neck. I remember my mother's stories about how often she moved when she was a child (and think about how she lived in the same house for 45 years). Gee,

19

James Breig

the wrong move by either one of them and I wouldn't be writing this.

Not long ago, a stranger wrote to me about my father because he recognized my name. He took the trouble to share a story from his teenage years when he met my father, then a reporter for a daily newspaper in Pittsburgh. They talked for a while, and my dad asked the teen what Catholic publications he read.

"I confessed, 'None,'" the man wrote me. "So your father asked when I expected to be in Pittsburgh again, and I gave him a date. When I did visit him again, he pulled out a huge paper box loaded with about 100 different periodicals. You should have seen this 90-pound teenager struggling with a 75-pound box of publications. We continued to correspond for about twenty years. He followed my career closely, all the while exhorting me to stay in the secular press."

I had never heard the story before; I'll treasure it now, especially for the irony it contains. My father left the daily newspaper to spend four decades in religious journalism.

The next time you get the urge to lecture with a wagging finger and screwed-up face, relax; sit down with your child and say, "You know what happened to me when I was your age?" You'll have an all-ears audience.

Where were you when Kennedy was killed?

I had just finished gym and arrived at my next class, high-school English, when the announcement was made: President Kennedy had been shot and killed in Dallas.

I remember thinking, like everyone else, "I will never forget this day." (I didn't know that, six years later, my first son would

Finding God in Your House

be born on November 22, changing the meaning of that date forever.)

The remainder of that afternoon unfolded silently. Classmates spoke in whispers; people seemed to walk softly; the air somehow was heavier.

When the school bus dropped me off, I sloped into my home and said to my mother, "Now I know why people get drunk."

She pointed to the dining room. That morning, deliverymen had dropped off a chord organ that she and my father had bought as a surprise to encourage my newfound interest in music.

The phrase "mixed emotions" cannot capture how she and I felt standing there, emptied by Dallas on a day when I should have been whooping with joy and filling the house with music, no matter how ineptly played.

For her sake, I sat down and pressed a few keys, sounding out a melody while trying to look pleased. But there was no joy in it, no energy, no sense of creativity.

When the news media recently marked the anniversary of the assassination of Bobby Kennedy, the son who was born on November 22 turned to me and asked, "Was he related in any way to John Kennedy?"

I could only stare at him. His brother, a year younger, scoffed. "You're such an idiot," he said. So I gestured to him and opened a trapdoor: "Okay, you tell your brother if they were related."

He smiled at his superior intelligence and replied, "Of course not."

Years after an event that had devastated me, my children did not know that the Kennedys who died were brothers. I do not blame them for this. After all, JFK, to them, is as obscure a president as Hoover and FDR are to me. Time marches on and the world spins.

And quiet afternoons of mixed emotions become lost in history.

Make teen faith a family affair

A lot of parents ask themselves this question: How can I help my teens to practice their faith and to live Catholic morality in a world which is intent on undermining everything I do? And what happens to my adolescents if I fail?

Those are scary questions because they go beyond the usual parental concerns about physical health, future employment, marriage preparation, college placement, or how to get a driver's license without banging up the family wagon. Those questions reach into the heart and soul, and involve the ultimate purposes for which we all were created.

Big questions, big worries. But God gave teens a big weapon: parents. I'm a firm believer in the power of parenting, even when it seems that it fails or when it requires all sorts of hollering and argumentation. The problem is that too many moms and dads get caught up in the daily (really, the hourly) struggle to keep their children on the right path. As a result, they cannot see the big picture or project into the future. That leads to frustration. And often, parents forget their own questioning, their own disbelief, their own doubts, their own struggle to find God—and that makes children feel hopeless in the face of parents who come off as perfect.

I know that is something that concerns parents because I do the same thing: I worry about this particular weekend and how much I am going to have to harangue my sons to get them to go to Mass with the rest of the family. In my worry, I forget that I, too, was lazy and wanted to roll over in bed, wanted to go on my own or sneaked out right after Communion. I also forget that my parents' efforts paid off in the long run—or I wouldn't be so concerned now about going to Mass as a family unit.

That being said, I'd like to offer some suggestions to parents on how to meet those everyday problems. These are just suggestions, I stress; I'm not an expert, I'm just a dad. My success won't be measured for decades to come, so I invite criticism, adjustments, adaptations and even rejection of these ideas by parents. But I also invite parents to make sure they do something to keep their teens aware that religion is important and that God exists.

Here are my suggestions:

1. **Practice what you preach.** Teens can be yammered at all you want; but if you don't do what you tell them to do, you are not going to get very far. If dad insists that his 16-year-old go to Mass every week while he sits at home, the child gets a very strong message, and it's not about the value of weekly communion with God or fellow Catholics. Parents also have to practice the other aspects of their religion which are not liturgical; aspects like justice, love, forgiveness, understanding, and tolerance. A mother who preaches love to her children and then signs a petition against a home for the retarded in the neighborhood sends a mixed message.

2. **Know what you are talking about.** If you haven't learned anything about religion, morality, ethics or spirituality since you last cracked a textbook, don't start to spread your ignorance around. Find resources (Christian book stores, parish religious

education materials, priests, nuns, brothers, permanent deacons) that can help you educate yourself. If you donate ignorance to your children, you have achieved very little. At the same time, don't be afraid to admit your ignorance on a certain subject and then seek out the answer to share it with your child.

3. **Be aware of what your children currently learn.** Study their religion textbooks whether they are in a Catholic school or attend religious education classes. Support their teachers, back up the lessons, offer to answer questions.

4. **Try sneak attacks.** I am often accused of delivering lengthy sermons through a stained-glass throat, a habit which causes even my wife to roll her eyes. While I endorse such formal lectures on occasion, I also know the value of the sneak attack. Small lessons in religion and morality can be delivered at opportune times when teens least expect or recognize it. But the message still gets through. I find that TV can provide endless opportunities for discussion of moral issues, especially sexual morality. After the family watches a show, begin a discussion on the issues contained in it. Don't lecture—and don't scoff at the teenager's response.

5. **Make your home a place where religion is a normal part of the routine.** Pray together, read the Bible, subscribe to Catholic periodicals, talk about God as often as baseball, be responsive to the signals which children put out that concern deeper issues. Young people want to know about sexual morality, praying, finding God and being a good person; but, frequently, they don't feel comfortable enough to speak about such matters. Try to make them comfortable, or at least be sensitive to the clues they give which indicate they want to know something.

6. **Don't be afraid to fail.** The best parents can produce the

Finding God in Your House

worst children. But it is more likely that your efforts will pay off sometime down the line. For a time, Junior may seem like the O'Hair-apparent, but odds are that he will straighten out. God works in mysterious ways and it sometimes takes a while for his hand to show up in a person's life. One needs only to study the lives of many saints to recognize that. (Imagine how Saint Monica felt about her boy Augustine; or, for that matter, what Joseph and Mary thought about their 30-year-old son who had yet to start his work.) If you can say that you made a significant effort to keep your children aware of God and the church, and the importance of living a moral life, then you have done your part. And, of course, you can continue to influence them through your prayers on their behalf after they have left the nest.

7. **Be strong enough to admit that you are a sinner.** Teens are well aware of their own failings, but parents can often give the impression that they themselves are immaculate. Share stories about your own weaknesses and failures, recall times when you struggled with faith, confess your own temptations.

Those are my suggestions. Use what's worthwhile, discard what isn't, adapt what needs changing—but do something. That's what parents are for.

(Excerpted from an article which first appeared in *Our Sunday Visitor.*)

Six o'clock sex talk

Many adults complain that their parents never taught them about sex. They then admit that they didn't teach their kids either. My experience was somewhat different. I remember my father addressing the topic at the kitchen table as we sat chatting one evening after everyone else had gone about their business.

He began with the physical details. He was, like most parents, too late with those. I had already put one and one together and had a rough idea of what went where. It's pretty obvious when you think about it, and preteen boys think about it a lot.

What I remember more, however, is my father's almost poetic description of marital love, including sex. He talked about passion and embracing and fidelity and commitment. He even managed to bring in the inventor of sex, God, without making him the divine spoilsport so many would have us believe in.

My dad's words were in my head when my wife, Mary, and I explained the facts of life (sexual department) to our two older children. I made sure to answer all their plumbing questions. The difference in generations was obvious when their questions covered such topics as transvestites, AIDS and venereal disease. Those are some public issues in the sexual area today; in my prehistoric time, the topics were much tamer.

Then, after the hardware was discussed, I could hear my father's words coming back to me as I spoke to them about marriage, the significance of sex in an age of trivialized mating, the value of virginity and the joys of marital love.

Did it work? I guess you and I will have to read my sons' newsletters in the next century to find out. I do know that my father's words must have contributed to my marriage and my ever-increasing love for my wife.

Thanks, Dad.

Beyond sex and violence: three more reasons not to watch TV

Recently I got tired of hearing myself lecture my kids about the sex and violence on television and why that content should make some programs out-of-bounds for viewing. Those twin reasons are the ones most frequently cited by parents, critics, boycotters and others who attack TV. Once I shut myself up about those two for a while, however, I started thinking about three other things on TV that Christians should object to. Maybe families need to start paying attention to this trio:

1. **Materialism:** Church leaders have identified this as one of the most harmful forces at work in the world. Yet viewers often don't consider it when they select their viewing for the night. Commercials, of course, are based entirely on materialism. And the fabric of many series is woven from materialism. Subtly, these programs can program us to crave yachts and mansions rather than what's really good for us.

Why should Catholic families care if materialism creeps into their lives through the Zenith? Check out Matthew 6:19-24.

2. **Power:** This force is linked with materialism because wealth often leads to one human being controlling another or one class dominating another. TV frequently celebrates power in such shows as "Lifestyles of the Rich and Famous," news profiles of world leaders, and fictional presentations that hold up dominating people as ones we should emulate.

Why should Catholic families care about a love of power being beamed at them by the Magnavox? Read Mark 9:33-37.

3. **Ridicule:** By far, the most common joke on television these days is the put-down. You can't watch any comedy series for long without hearing one character make fun of another's size, habits, appearance, abilities or demeanor. For the most part, television has abandoned the ethnic slur and the racial stereotype. In their place, the tube has substituted humor that attacks individuals rather than groups. Mom insults the kids and Dad;

James Breig

the kids insult each other; Dad insults Mom's relatives; coworkers insult one another.

But so what? Why should Christians be bothered by such one-liners? I refer you, for an answer, to John 13:34-35.

Materialism, power and ridicule are three powerful forces on television; and they have nothing to do with sex or violence. There are other forces I could have listed: greed, sexism, racism, anti-religious sentiment and an adoration of trivia.

TV is powerful, influential and beaming hour after hour into practically every home in America. In most homes, families will have to search for a Bible to find the references above; but they know precisely what day, time and channel to find even the crudest shows.

Know their peers

I remember clearly a conversation I had with my mother when I was a first- or second-grader. If you grew up in a cold climate, I'll bet you had the same debate. (I wonder what kids in Florida argue with their moms about.) It went like this:

Mom: "Don't forget to wear your hat outside. It's cold."

Me: "Aw, Mom, I don't wanna. None of the guys wear hats."

Mom: "If all the guys jumped off the Empire State Building, would you do it, too?"

The reason I recall this discussion is simple: it has occurred more recently with me taking the "mom" role and my own children playing the part of me. (By the way, I substitute a local bridge for the Empire State Building, a touch that I foolishly think will have persuasive effect.)

The child's compulsion to do "Y" when mom and daddy

28

Finding God in Your House

say "X" results from peer pressure, the power exerted by same-age people over one another. (When we're adults, we call it "keeping up with the Joneses," which is simply another way of caving in to peer pressure.) When we're younger, our parents wonder where we get our wacky ideas about dressing weirdly, combing our hair oddly, or hanging out in bizarre locales. The ideas, of course, come from friends, who begin to have more and more influence over children as soon as they get beyond toddlerhood.

From one parent (me) to all of you, here are ten ideas, suggestions, guidelines and one-liners about peer pressure to help you deal with it in your home. These come from my experience, reading and reflection: take what works for you, adapt some others and reject those which have no relevance.

1. Don't assume that all peers are useless. A recent article in *Parents* magazine lists some of the beneficial outcomes of peer influence. Thanks to friends, the article explains, children get emotional support, an outlet for their anger, acceptance and role models for such virtues as generosity, empathy and helpfulness. So peer pressure can sometimes be pressure for the good.

2. Therefore, be aware of who your children's friends are. Don't go by looks; one of my son's best friends wears an earring, long hair and rather strange garb. First impressions were less than thrilling; but he has turned out to be a good friend, a welcome guest in our home and totally unlike our guess as to what he was.

Get to know the peer group. Drive the kids to functions, take them out for pizza, treat them to a ball game. You don't have to intrude or be a nuisance to become aware of the friends who influence your youngsters.

3. Give your children the language they need to resist peer pressure when it's harmful. Dr. Thomas Lickona in his book *Raising Good Children* writes, "Often, kids will resist peer pressure if they can just think of a way to say no and still be 'cool.' . . . You can help them think of words to say when they face tough situations." So project what temptations peers might offer your youngsters and discuss those occasions with them.

4. Don't give up. It's easy for moms and dads to fold their cards and say, "I've had it; that's enough." Resist that urge. It's the easy way out; but, in the long run, it won't help your children or you. Keep plugging away. For all the frustrations and lack of immediate rewards, parents need to keep at it. More and more studies conclude that parents have much more influence over their children than their children care to admit or let on about. You're succeeding, so plunge back into the fray.

5. If trouble comes, don't be afraid to seek help. Parents often get bogged down in the feeling of "my kids are the only ones who ever did that." You can find help in therapy groups, counseling, church organizations and other places. And don't forget your own peers. Chances are you can find other couples (including your own parents) who have gone through similar situations and who have good advice on surviving, coping and moving forward.

6. When you fight a battle, make sure it's worth fighting. All parents have to decide for their own families what rules are important. Waging loud and long fights over minor problems leaves little room for emphasizing major issues when they come along.

7. Let go. Realize that your children are not you. They want

to dress differently, listen to different music, hold different views. While they may do so by copying peers as a starter, chances are that they will eventually develop their own interests; and it's very likely that those will gravitate back toward you.

8. Remember that your child is some other child's peer and, therefore, some other parent's worry. While you check how friends influence your youngsters, be sure to pay attention to how your kid influences others.

9. As the twig is bent . . . Children watch parents for lessons in how to behave. What's your example as far as friendship is concerned? Do you copy the bad habits of peers? Who influences you? What can your child learn by observing your behavior?

10. Don't neglect prayer. Consider the list of saints who have dealt with peer pressure on various levels: Augustine, Maria Goretti, Thomas Merton, Kateri Tekakwitha, Paul. The Blessed Mother knows what it was like to raise a child; and that child himself faced temptation from the devil as well as from his own followers, who frequently suggested that he could tone down his teachings. Solace, guidance and encouragement can be sought through prayer on both the personal level and as a family group.

(Thanks to my friends at *Our Sunday Visitor* for allowing me to excerpt this from an article I wrote for them.)

Let go and rejoice

Jesus was never a parent, but he often had to deal with his disciples as if they were children. They showed several signs of immaturity: constant bickering, confusion, doubt. Remember when Jesus was trying to calm them down? They had panicked because he informed them that he was going away. This threw them into a tizzy.

"Do not be distressed or fearful," he reassured them. "You have heard me say, 'I go away for a while and I come back to you.' If you truly loved me, you would rejoice to have me go to the Father."

It occurs to me that parents could be told the same thing by children who are about to enter college or get married or leave home for a new job or move out of state. Letting go can be one of the most difficult things for parents to do. After having their children in their grasp and sight for two decades, parents eventually have to send them out into the world.

If parents were perfect people, they would rejoice, wish them luck, and be fully confident that they would return. But parents are not perfect. And neither are their kids. So, instead of rejoicing, parents worry. And, instead of coming back, children forget their parents' address.

When children go off on their own, it should be a time of joy. More often, it is a time of worry and tears and sadness.

This is easy for me to say, of course. My kids are still at home. You see, what I'm doing, don't you? I'm trying to talk myself into it. Sure, I'll be joyful at parting, and I won't worry and I'll be eager to wave good-bye.

Sure.

CHAPTER 2

Life with my Mary

No lights, no camera, lots of action

A pet theory of mine goes like this: make a 60-second commercial of everyone's life and we'll all be envious of ourselves.

Let me explain.

If you're like me, you envy the people in commercials on television. They walk in slow motion; they have glistening smiles; their day is filled with soft music and wonderful light; they never have any flaws.

Of course, the people in commercials aren't real. The actors are real; and, if we saw their lives, we wouldn't be envious. As they film an ad, they are probably exhausted, too cold or too hot, cranky over some delay, angry with the director, and upset over how the makeup has failed to hide their cold sore. But the people they play aren't real. If they were, a comment like "ring around the collar" would earn them a fat lip, the women in the exercise tights would sweat and have love handles, and the men in the beer commercials would smell bad.

Still, my wife, Mary, and I can often be heard saying, as we watch the tube, "Why can't life be like that?"

I believe it could be like that if some enterprising video company would offer to make 60-second commercials of our lives. We could be made up so that our acne doesn't show, and filmed in slow motion so that our gait would be elegant and graceful. Background music would complement our activities as we kissed well-behaved children goodbye in the morning, dallied at the office with smiling co-workers, and arrived home sunny and eager for a night on the town. It would take a lot of editing, but it could be done.

Recently, I invited Mary to try a "movie experience" in real life. She has often wondered why we don't stroll barefoot on the beaches or dine on balconies where the wind moves only enough to stir the edge of your hair. So when a snowstorm hit our town, dumping several inches of shiny white stuff on the ground, I seized the chance. She had said good night a few minutes before I got the idea, so I had to roust her from bed.

"Let's go for a walk in the snow," I said brightly.

She eyed the clock. "It's 10 p.m."

"Come on," I urged. "You always want to be like the movies. In the movies, the couple would go out for a stroll; and you would watch and say, "We never do that.' Come on."

"If I hadn't already got undressed . . ." she began.

I could tell she needed only a little more prodding. "It'll be romantic," I said.

To my surprise (getting Mary out of bed once she has retired is like extricating me from a ball game after the first pitch), she clambered out and started dressing.

Our children looked at us with that "whatta cuppla wackos" expression that only children can muster. We donned coats, hats, gloves and scarves and braved the storm.

The neighborhood was bright with the snow. "It's like afternoon," Mary said, her voice filled with wonder.

We held hands and began our circle of the block, admiring

how the snow clung to tree branches and how the light from homes seemed so dreamlike as it streamed through the frosty air. As our feet crunched the drifts beneath street lamps, the shadows of falling snow sprinkled around us.

We paused in the middle of the street to kiss and moved on when someone opened a door to peer out at the nuts who would be out walking on a night like this.

When we returned home, to make sure our kids could testify to our lack of sanity, we did what any movie characters would do at that point: we built a snowman.

If someone had filmed us that night and shown it on TV, millions of people would have envied us and said, "It only happens in the movies."

But not always. Sometimes, it happens in real life, too. I recommend it if you ever get the chance. And the movies you'll have in your head can be rerun endlessly.

But what if my wife wants carpeting?

The Pope is ruining my marriage. So are the American bishops. Not with their comments on birth control or sexuality or the education of our children. They are doing it by issuing challenging, disturbing documents on the Christian obligation to help the poor.

They want me to help the needy. But my wife wants carpeting.

The bishops did it first with their pastoral on the economy, which says, among other things, that "at times, we will be called upon to say no to the cultural manifestations that emphasize values and aims that are selfish, wasteful, and opposed to the Scriptures. Together, we must reflect on our personal and family

35

decisions, and curb unnecessary wants in order to meet the needs of others. . . . All of us could well ask ourselves whether, as a Christian prophetic witness, we are not called to adopt a simpler lifestyle in the face of the excessive accumulation of material goods that characterizes an affluent society."

Then along came John Paul II with his encyclical "On Social Concerns." In it, he writes, "Just as one may sin through selfishness and the desire for excessive profit and power, one may also be found wanting with regard to the urgent needs of multitudes of human beings submerged in conditions of underdevelopment through fear, indecision and, basically, through cowardice. We are all called, indeed obliged, to face the tremendous challenge of the last decade of the second millennium. . . . At stake is the dignity of the human person, whose defense and promotion have been entrusted to us by the Creator, and to whom the men and women of every moment of history are strictly and responsibly in debt."

But my wife wants carpeting.

Most Americans live in luxury when they compare their lives to the billions of people around the world who have little or nothing. For all my whining about taxes, mortgage rates, electric bills and medical costs, we have a stable government, housing, heat and health care. How many people have died for the lack of those in the time it has taken me to write this paragraph and you to read it? Is it right . . . is it just . . . is it moral . . . is it Christian . . . is it following Jesus . . . for so few to have so much of the world's goods and not to share them more?

The Pope and the bishops say it is not right, and they have Scripture on their side. But Mary wants carpeting.

Finding God in Your House

And so we argue. We've lived in our house for ten years, she says, and the carpeting was shot when we moved in. It's time to get new floor coverings. But, I respond, "there are starving families in Ethiopia and homeless children in Colombia and cardboard shantytowns in the Far East. How can we write a check for hundreds of dollars to make our floors look nicer when those people have so little?"

And she answers: "we sponsor two children overseas, we give to every collection for every charity; we support organizations that seek to change the system, we raise our children to be sensitive to the needs of others. Carpeting for us is not a sin."

Then I wonder: Am I just being cheap? Am I using the poor as an excuse not to part with money? Is it my wife's desires that I deny while justifying my own purchases? And how do I draw the line? What is luxury and what is necessity? What is for comfort and what is for aggrandizement? How much can we put away for our future retirement needs when so many have present needs? Am I forcing my wife to play the role of philistine as I cast myself as true believer when, in reality, she is the one who reaches out to others in need? I can write checks, but she takes food to ailing neighbors and comforts our friends when they're upset about something.

Jesus came to bring the sword; and his followers, the bishops and the Pope, have been swinging it rather freely in my home lately.

So I pray: Lord, I want to follow you; I want to share with the poor; I believe that we have an obligation to help the less fortunate, the least of your brothers and sisters. But my wife wants carpeting. So what do I do?

I eagerly await your answer.

James Breig

A night at the movies

There's one sure way to get a groan from visitors to your home: say, "Let's look at some home movies!"

But I found just the opposite reaction recently when a handful of circumstances came together to create a memorable night of 8mm viewing.

I've taken home movies for more than 20 years, first with the families of my siblings when I was a teenager and then with my own family. Over the years I've built up a sizable stack of reels. But a few years ago, the projector broke. So the films sat on a shelf, unseen.

Then, when my mother and sister came for a visit recently, I had a brainstorm. I bought a projector and suggested we dig out the old films—and some new ones that had been developed but never shown.

Since we were all relatives, there was no chance of boring neighbors and friends who find home movies a yawn because they don't know the people in them or the circumstances. The six of us who gathered in the darkened family room knew the cast of characters. The result was a perfect evening of laughter, tears, and memories.

My wife got misty over the shots of babies who are now adolescents. . . . My mother wanted us to find the short (no more than 10 seconds) section that showed her father, now dead more than two decades. . . . My son, embarrassed over evidence of him in diapers and the odd little suits parents think are cute, kept repeating, "I look slick" with just the right sarcasm. . . . My daughter wondered when we would get to the late '70s and her arrival. . . .

Finding God in Your House

Halfway through, we stopped to make popcorn and sort out the good ones we wanted to put aside to show the son who was absent that night. I wish he had been there to hear his mother's comments. Her love for him and his brother and sister resounded in her voice as she kept repeating the chant, "Look at them." Those three words said, "I can't believe how the years have passed" and "Remember how cute they were as babies" and "I don't remember growing older" and "Do you know how much I care for you?" and "I wish dealing with teenagers were as easy as plopping a toddler into a sandbox" and "Please don't lose all your childhood innocence."

I felt very close to my family that night—my own family and my parents', the ones in the room with me and the ones who are now images on a screen.

If you haven't looked at home movies or slides or photos recently, see if you can hit the right moment to bring them out. Reminisce with the youngsters about the old days, yours and theirs. Connections can be made via those celluloid images and the stories that go with them.

Pick you up at 8

My wife went out on a date the other night. Her escort came to the house and picked her up, leaving behind flowers for her and two rosebuds for her daughter, and some soft drinks for the boys to enjoy since they would be stuck at home babysitting.

My sons looked at the man with quizzical turns of their heads. They couldn't quite figure out who he was.

The evening included dinner for two and then attendance at a performance by a popular comedian.

39

James Breig

Before you start to worry, I'd better add that I was the man and that my sons were puzzled that I would drive up to the house after work, ring the doorbell, speak politely to everyone and ask them their names and ages.

That morning, I had called my wife to ask her out, telling her the time and appropriate attire (previously, of course, I had informed my sons of the idea so they would be home to take care of their sister). Then I stayed away from the house until it was the appointed hour.

It sounds a little weird, I'll admit, but it works. My wife and I did this once before—a post-marital date—and it worked out great. She got to recall the days when she eagerly waited for someone to come to the door; I got to buy flowers and make plans. We acted like youngsters in the first blush of love, and it was good to recapture that feeling.

You husbands might like to give it a try. (And, ladies, don't be too shy to reverse the order if he won't go for it.)

Keep that honeymoon feeling

My wife Mary and I did something recently which was dangerous, untried, potentially disastrous and fraught with unknown terrors.

We returned to the same place we went on our honeymoon. The place is Williamsburg, Virginia, where a restored colonial city is the main attraction. Since we both love early American art and design, and she has a special fascination for antiques, it was the perfect spot for a honeymoon back in the late '60s. Since Mary continues to love antiques and continues to love me, I decided to treat her to a return visit to those thrilling days of yesteryear.

We both had our doubts about returning to the scene of the crime. For almost two decades, Williamsburg had held a special place in our memories, and we worried that we could ruin all that by going back older, different, and burdened with all those years of children, bills, work, and—we admit it—arguments. To see a place with love's first blush cannot be duplicated. What would it be like to return with that blush somewhat pale on our cheeks?

In preparation, we fished out the scrapbook that I had made after our honeymoon. Mary got the sniffles as we paged through the photos and memorabilia. I had pasted into the book all sorts of trifles, like hotel bills ($17 for a room! Yipes!) and ticket stubs. Each item brought back a rush of happy memories for simpler times when it was just the two of us. Might going back mean destroying those memories? We both knew it was a risk.

But the risk paid off, and handsomely. When we returned, friends would ask how it went; and I would reply, "Perfect." I think Mary agrees. The weather was fine, the food and lodging great, the sight-seeing fun. But, above all that, there was the renewed closeness between us, a closeness that comes partially from removing three children who tend to keep us apart but which also derives from recapturing honeymoon feelings.

We held hands, kissed in public and talked for hours without interruption. We remembered certain exhibits and places and buildings, all of which flooded us with nostalgia. We were like old folks recalling the golden days, telling people, "We were here years ago," as if they would care. And it felt good. It was like going home, not to a place but to a moment and an emotion and a promise.

James Breig

Of course, it had to end despite those constant questions to each other: "Do we have to leave? Can't we move here? Why don't we stay another week?" The glow fades and the routine returns, but I think the experience has had a lasting effect. I know one thing: we won't wait years to go back—if not to the place, then at least to the feeling.

Staying married takes a lot of words

A friend got married recently. As I sat beside my wife, Mary, at the nuptial Mass, I thought what I would tell my friend if she asked what has kept Mary and me together. I think I would have replied:

"Be flexible. Be willing to compromise. But, most of all, be willing to ask for and to give forgiveness."

Mary and I have fought, as all couples do. We've had our silent days. Each of us has stomped out of the house to drive around for a while, cooling off. But we both have the willingness to say, "I'm sorry; how about you?"

The mutuality of sorrow is important, I believe. In fact, it has become something of a joke between us. When we're mad at each other, I'll eventually go up to Mary and say, "I forgive you," even though she has not yet said she's sorry or—more often—even though I may be the one at fault. Mary will smile at my big-hearted ability to admit she's wrong, and then we'll sort out what made us angry, kiss and make up.

I suppose there are a thousand things that contribute to a happy marriage, but that's what I was thinking about when my friend said, "I do."

Finding God in Your House

I never knew love like this before

Mary and I recently celebrated our twentieth wedding anniversary.

That should be followed by a humble sentence that reads: Thanks to Mary, our marriage has lasted. But that would be only half true. I'm un-humble enough to claim part of the credit. Our marriage has lasted thanks to us.

Thanks to us, we never let arguments last too long. I think our record might have been three days of chilly silence before we sat down and worked out whatever it was that had divided us.

Thanks to us, we always remembered what was important to each other. I never forgot her birthday. She always remembered how much I love brownies.

Thanks to us, we overcame differences in taste (why can't she like baseball—just a teeny bit?) and personality (she often wondered if the word "sociable" had been left out of my formative years).

Thanks to us, we held fast to the love while shooing away the negative things that confront all couples.

We've made it this far together. Thanks to us. And we, in turn, have to thank our parents for showing us how, our children for giving us three more reasons to love, our church for insisting that we try harder, and our God for blessing us in every imaginable way.

Poets and songs say that love is eternal. Mary and I have put in two decades of eternity, and I am looking forward to the remainder of our time as one. I've written her songs and she's baked me cakes. I've bought her flowers and she's bought me baseball books (even though they only encourage me to watch more games on TV). Most of all, we've brought each other love. There have been spats and silent treatments, disputes and cold spells. But, most of all, there has been love.

Every Christmas, I leave Mary a love letter in her stocking. It's a way of wishing her a happy holiday, of celebrating our December 21 anniversary, and of wrapping up the previous year. The letter I left this time was special. I've shared a lot with readers, but some things are too private. So I'll leave you guessing on the contents.

But the stocking was stuffed with twenty years of love.

Till death do us part

This book is based on factual situations and real-life occurrences. But I thought it might be fun to try a little fiction in the form of a short parable about marriage.

Once upon a time, there were a husband and wife who loved each other very much. They always tried to do things for each other. He made her breakfast; she made his lunch; they went out for dinner. When she was sick, he nursed her. When he was ill, she doctored him. When the flu got them both, they moaned in unison and loved holding each other.

They were together in all things. Except for one. The husband prayed each night that, when his time came, he would die quickly, quietly, and while his wife was out so that she would not have to see him suffer. She would not be able to stand that, he thought, because she loves me so much.

The years rolled on. They made breakfasts and lunches and nursed and doctored until they looked in the mirror and saw

Finding God in Your House

gray in place of jet black, wrinkles where smoothness once lay, and a stoop instead of a straight back.

And the man got sick, and she doctored him; but he didn't get better. He couldn't get up to make breakfast, he wouldn't eat his lunch, and he was asleep by dinnertime. The days and weeks went on as he weakened, declined and moved toward death.

His prayers grew more fervent: quickly, quietly, and while she's out, he prayed; don't let her see me suffer. She is not strong enough; it will destroy her.

Then his final day came. As his breathing became more labored and his eyelids drooped, she crawled into bed with him, slid her arm around his shoulders, and pulled him closer than ever.

"God is not good," he whispered. "I have prayed all my life that I would not die in your arms. And now this. God does not answer prayers."

She smiled, kissed him one last time, and said, "Yes, he does. Because, all my life, I have had one prayer every night: let my husband die in my arms so that he does not leave me without a goodbye kiss."

CHAPTER 3

Our family portrait

In whose image?

I'm thinking about going back through all my records and adding up what I've spent on religious education during the lifetime of my teenage son, Jimmy. Then I'm going to demand a refund.

The cause of my desperation is a conversation he and I had one night as we flipped around the TV dial. We hit on a show that purported to find the geographical location of the Garden of Eden.

"Were Adam and Eve real people?" he asked.

"I don't think so," I replied.

"Noah?"

"I don't know. But it doesn't matter. The Bible isn't *The New York Times*. It's trying to tell us about God's creation and his love for us, not the facts of who, what, when and where."

I thought I was doing well.

"Do you believe in creation or evolution?" he continued.

"Both." This astonished him. "I believe God created the world, but I don't know how he did it. Science thinks that evolution was the method. It doesn't matter. What matters is that God exists and he made all that is."

Now I knew I was doing great. I nominated myself for Father of the Year.

Finding God in Your House

"Tell me this," he said. "If we're made in God's image, does he look like us or like prehistoric man?"

I just stared in disbelief. Then I clicked off the TV.

"Uh-oh," he moaned, "this is going to be a long answer, isn't it?"

I nodded. . . .

When I told this story to a woman who works with families, she said my son was thinking creatively and applying his book-learning to everyday life.

"That's good," she told me. "He's showing that what he learned by rote he is now thinking about."

I nodded and smiled.

Then she gave me a pretty good shot by telling me about another father who was lecturing at the dinner table and stopped when he noticed his son was daydreaming.

"Pay attention," he ordered.

"The trouble with you, Dad," said the boy, "is that when you talk, you expect everybody to take notes."

Touché.

But I still want my money back.

That first step is a big one

First Carrie and her brother Matt borrowed Jimmy's watch to play track meet. Then Carrie dropped the watch and broke the glass. So Jimmy took Carrie's deely-boppers (remember those?) and deliberately busted them in retaliation. Next Carrie cried, and Jimmy was sent to his room to think it over.

Whew!

When he reappeared among civilized humans, I said, "That

was a horrible thing to do."

"I know it," he said.

Three little words, but they showed his growing maturity. It's not easy for adults to admit they are wrong; to see it in someone his age over something so silly impressed me. It's difficult to own up to being weak, human and sinful. That's why the reconciliation rooms are not overflowing. Inevitably, after someone admits they are at fault, they feel better because they are unburdened of guilt and welcomed back into the family. But that first step is not taken without pain. Self-awareness and maturity are two of the goodies which come with that step, however; so it is worth sticking a foot out.

A comet by the tale

I first heard about Halley's Comet when I was a little kid. Again and again my father would regale me with stories about the comet that visited here when he was a child. He told me how blazingly bright it was, so bright that it could be seen in the daytime, and seemingly so close to the earth that children of that time worried it would smash into the world.

My father longed to see Halley's again, but he died before its return. When it got close in 1986, I shared his tales with my children. One of my sons, Jimmy, made a special request that we drive to the country to see the comet on a cloudless night away from the city lights.

"When it comes back again," he said, "I want to be able to tell people I saw it when I was little."

He'll be 92 when it zooms back. We pondered if he would make it that far. I won't. But the connections go on. There's

Finding God in Your House

the famous story about Mark Twain, who was born in a Halley year and then died when it returned—the year my father saw it . . . who passed on the story to me . . . and I passed it on to my children . . . and the cycle goes on and on.

I'm a believer in telling stories from the past to children. No matter how much they pretend to be bored or really are, the stories stick and make connections and solidify a family. Those boring stories of today become heirlooms for the future to be handed on.

When my son is 92 and tells his grandkids about Halley's, he'll tell them about me and my father and Mark Twain. And they'll start counting to see how old the youngest will be when the comet comes back again.

Now hear this

"I feel like such a jerk."

It isn't often a teenager will utter those words in public and to his entire family. So my ears perked up one night at dinner when my son, Matt, 14, spoke that sentence as he cleared away the dishes.

Teens, who are filled with self-doubt, self-accusation and low self-esteem like to put on a much more confident front. They will tell you all the time how good they are, how strong they are and how much they look like Tom Cruise—assuming, of course, they are boys.

So for Matt to say, "I feel like such a jerk," was an extraordinary confession. He went on to tell what happened along his newspaper route when he went collecting.

"There's this one house where no one will ever answer the

doorbell,'' he said. ''They ignore me all the time because they don't want to pay me. I can hear them in there and see lights on, but they never come to the door. One time, I could even see in the window, and I saw the old man. No matter how much I knocked and rang, he wouldn't get up. I figured he was a cheapskate, trying to cheat me.

''Then I found out he's deaf. I feel like such a jerk.''

For once, he didn't feel like a jerk because someone cheated him or because of something he did (like leaving the spoon in the applesauce jar when he puts it in the fridge). He felt like a jerk because of something he felt and thought.

I think that's a special sign of maturity: to recognize that our faults are not just actions but also attitudes.

A co-worker, a woman in her 50s, has often said that she doesn't think she ever sins. I think she defines sin as something done; since she doesn't ''do bad things,'' she doesn't sin. But what about attitudes toward others, thoughts about friends, beliefs about races, clichés about the poor? Those can be sins and ones that linger with us for years.

Congratulations, Matt, on another step toward adulthood. You're not a jerk at all.

To tell youth the truth

Carrie, my 9-year-old, and I were watching ''Highway to Heaven,'' a television program that I found to be a great resource to help start conversations.

The episode in question concerned a black woman who was pastor of a community church. Back into her life came a man who had loved her years earlier. Bitter over his leaving, she was cold to him now and ordered him to call her "Pastor" or "Reverend" but nothing more dear.

In the course of the show (and true love), he asked her to marry him. That's when Carrie said: "She can't marry him."

"Why not?" I asked.

"She's a pastor," she replied, logically. "Pastors can't get married."

Four things went through my mind rapidly. First I thought how nice it was that the character's race never entered into our discussion. I don't think I've ever heard Carrie make a remark that indicated she even notices the differences among races. A credit to her (and us?).

Next I realized that she was equating "pastor" with "priest" since the only priest in our parish is the pastor. Then I understood that she was not allowing for the possibility that the woman was not a Catholic. Finally I gulped over the recognition that the character's gender was not a consideration for Carrie.

What a wonderful tribute to her! She had erased all divisions among people, scoring points simultaneously for ecumenism, feminism and race relations.

What a horrible task for me! I had to introduce her to the realities of the world where religious divisions scandalize Christianity and where regulations keep women from the altar.

After I spoke about the church's men-only policy regarding the priesthood, Carrie demanded, "Who made that rule?"

"Some say Jesus," I explained, "because he picked only men to be his Apostles. Other people say there were women priests after he died. The popes have kept the rule."

And, keeping it, I wonder what effect this will have on Carrie if she does have a vocation.

James Breig

I like teaching my children about the world, but I don't always like the information I have to convey.

When is a Porsche not a Porsche?

Like all fathers, I am prone to giving lectures. In the past, I would surreptitiously try to introduce my profound thoughts into my kids' day. But they soon recognized what I was up to and their requisite groan would follow. You know the groan; it begins, "Aw, Dad, not again."

So I gave up. No, I didn't stop lecturing; I was just more aboveboard about it. I would tell my children to sit down and grin 'n' bear it because here comes a lecture. "You might as well pretend to like it," I would say, "because your groaning will only make it longer."

Whether my orations were overt or covert, I never knew if they were getting through. But, every now and then, a piece of evidence turns up to indicate that the message was received and filed for future reference. The latest clue to surface came from my teenage son Matt. Years ago, he was a favorite target of my lectures because he was getting into minor scrapes at school and home.

Lecture #1 was delivered when he would complain about going to church every Sunday and went like this: "If I offered to give you $168 and all you had to do was give me a buck, would you make the trade?" Unsuspecting, he would nod vigorously. Then I would spring the trap: "Well, that's God's offer to you: 168 hours a week for one hour on Sunday at Mass. It's a pretty good deal."

Lecture #2 would follow low grades: "What if a friend of

yours got a Porsche, which you loved? And what if he were going away for a while and asked you to take care of it for him? Would you agree? And would you make sure it was polished and cared for? Would you park it in a garage overnight and keep it safe? And what if the friend returned to find you had left it out in the rain and banged its bumpers and never changed the oil? Would he have a right to complain and feel that you let him down?''

Again, Matt would nod in agreement; his love for cars made this example very real to him. So, once more, the trapdoor dropped beneath his sneakered feet. ''Don't you see,'' I would say. ''God has given you a Porsche. He's given you brains and talent, but you're wasting them by not doing well in school.''

The scene dissolves; the years pass. Matt made it through grade school and high school and is now in college. The time: a Sunday in the present. The place: the dinner table. The characters: the entire family. As we finished our meal, Carrie, our 11-year-old, was asked why she didn't volunteer to become an altar server in our parish. She began her defense by listing all of the other activities that she is involved in: dancing lessons, basketball, Brownies. . . .

That's when Matt interrupted her and chimed in: ''Carrie, if I offered you $168 for $1 in return, would you take it?''

My mouth dropped open. My wife, Mary, laughed. Carrie just stared in confusion and tried to restart her explanation. But Matt wouldn't be denied. He cut her off again: ''Carrie, you're getting your Porsche all rusty.''

I sat back and sighed contentedly. Father's Day can sometimes come early and the gifts can sometimes be so satisfying.

James Breig

So I'll have to say 'I love you' in a letter

Mary has been threatening not to attend our firstborn's graduation from high school. For months now, she has been saying
that she knows she will break down and cry from the proces-
sional to the post-ceremony photos. Her threats are empty, of
course. But her prediction is not. She'll cry copiously, just as
she does at other such moments, from Jimmy's birth to his
brother's appearance in a school pageant to our daughter's ballet
recital.

My emotions tend to be masculine: I get tight in the throat
and maybe a little misty-eyed. This allows Mary to pretend that
I'm the solid one she can depend on at such moments to comfort her. Fortunately I have another release in writing. I can
put down in words what I'm feeling. Verbs are my tears; nouns
are my sniffles; sentences are my embraces.

So here are a few verbs nouns, and sentences about Jimmy,
in the form of an open letter to him as he leaves high school:

Dear Jimmy:

Highlight moments like graduations always recall similar
events. Like your birth in November 1969. But I can go back
even further—to the summer before, when your mother and I
lay in bed together watching Neil Armstrong land on the moon.
I remember looking at her and the bulge, which you formed
from inside her, and saying, "Our child will never know a time
when people didn't go into space." That was the first time I
felt old.

The fact that you were born on November 22 (after 20-plus
hours of labor that I'm glad I didn't go through) seemed ironic.

Finding God in Your House

That date for my generation always stood for one thing: John F. Kennedy's assassination. Now November 22 would mean something sublime rather than tragic.

Those were the days when fathers paced in waiting rooms at hospitals, watching for the arrival not of their children but of doctors informing them what had happened. It was around 7 a.m. when our doctor stepped off the elevator to tell me that you now existed outside your mother.

Between then and now there are so many memories: you throwing a tantrum because Mom would not buy you a trench-coat because she considered it a somewhat sophisticated garment for a first-grader . . . you dressed up for your First Communion (but that was nothing unusual; you wore a tie around the house and "shaved" with me every morning by using a wooden block as your razor). . . . the time you dove into the community swimming pool—the wrong way—and ended up on the pavement. I can feel you in my arms as I carried you to the car, and, of course, we still have photographic evidence of your fractured nose. Smart of you to do a one-point landing . . . your brother standing at the back door covered in mud because you "painted" him that way . . . your graduation from grade school, your Confirmation, your first dance, your first car (and how it broke down just hours after you got it).

I think of how your face has changed: from babyfat to pimples to whiskers. Of how your hands have grown, of how your mind has expanded, of how your goodness has begun to show through—not because we make you do things but because you want to do them: serve Mass, treat your sister to an ice cream cone, help a friend.

When your mother cries at your graduation, Jimmy, and you

see her love dampen her cheeks, remember that mine is equally there—not in tears but in verbs and nouns. "Love" is both. We love you.

Wait a second; he's first class

Here's an open letter to our second son, Matt, on his graduation from high school.

Dear Matt:

Our middle child, Matt. That's been your designation, and I know it's been a less than glamorous slot to fill in a family. There you are, stuck between first son and the first girl, between the firstborn and the baby.

It has been your lot in life to do everything a year later than your brother, who is just 11 months older than you. I know what it's like to follow in an older brother's shadow, but, in my case, that shadow was 6 years old by the time I caught up with it. It had faded some in that time.

So I don't envy the close distance you trail your brother, Jimmy. It means that our first experience of everything (first tooth, first Christmas, first kindergarten, first graduation) was with Jimmy. It's not Jimmy's fault; it's no one's fault. It's just the order in which we arrive in families.

But I wonder if you know the "firsts" you brought us. I wonder if we've told you all the pleasures, joys and delights you've given us in ways neither of the other kids did. When you parade down the commencement aisle, your mom and I will be remembering scenes like these:

• Our decision to name you Matthew Lawrence to honor (in your middle name) your mother's father. Where'd Matthew come from? It sounded good: Matt Breig. Like a linebacker. Like someone with substance. Solid. Like the way you turned out.

• The saintly self-sacrifice you displayed as a child. We remember times when we'd split a treat between you and Jimmy. When he'd finish his half and stare longingly at yours, you'd give it to him. We've seen that same sense of giving last through the years in the way you treat friends. You're there for them when they need you.

• Your declaration at the dinner table that, no matter what you grew up to be, you didn't want to become a "condominium." It took us a while to figure out you meant a "custodian." The one at school worked too hard, you figured and that wasn't the life for you.

• The line of clothing that you would leave on the way into the bathroom. Not to take a bath, just to go to the toilet, which, for some reason, you thought required complete nudity.

• Your constant efforts at construction, repair and design. There was the fort outside our bedroom window . . . the bikes in pieces in the basement . . . and those blocks you glued together in an effort to make a—well, what was that anyway?

• The time you ran away and hid under the fir tree across the street, contentedly watching your mother as she frantically searched the neighborhood for you.

• Your feelings for your girlfriend, Missy. I keep coming back to ideas of loyalty and solidity and constancy. Those virtues show up in how you and Missy treat each other. Going steady as teenagers can be a difficult process (and, sometimes, worrisome for parents), but you two have shown a fidelity that many married couples would do well to imitate.

- Your growing love of reading. While a certain other son is a couch potato, you've developed a reading habit that needs no cure. Sometimes I think you should turn that interest onto its flip side and try writing. Someday maybe you will. I'd like to see the results.

- Your sense of humor. We shouldn't spoil you with these admissions, but you're our funniest child. When you get going with one of your stories, complete with grimaces and gestures, you're a riot.

Those memories will be in our heads when you get your diploma; in our hearts will be the love we feel, a love that takes second place to no one. You're not our first, and none of our kids is the best. But you're the Matthew-est: handsome, funny, faithful and daring.

Any many more

The following is my letter to Carrie on the occasion of her eighth birthday:

Dear Carrie:

Your brothers say we spoil you because you're the baby and the only girl. They're probably right. Parents loosen up by the time the third one comes around; and girls, despite Gloria Steinem, are treated differently from boys.

But the real reason we spoil you is because we love you. Not the third child and not the girl, but you: Carrie. One reason we love you is that we have known you so long. In fact, we knew you before you were born. That's because we saw pictures of you when you were still inside your mother. There you were: a tiny shadow on a doctor's screen. You weren't named yet, and we didn't know you would be born with cheeks that looked like Dizzy Gillespie's; but we were in love with you.

And we haven't stopped loving you. Sometimes we get mad at you; and, sometimes, you get mad at us. But most of the time we don't; and, all of the time, we love you. That sounds crazy—loving someone when you are mad at them—but that's how parents and children are. It's also why parents and children try not to get too mad too often and to make up for it when they do.

You're getting to be a more mature young lady, despite the thumb in the mouth (don't worry; both your mom and I sucked away on our thumbs until we were older than you are now). You're smart in school, a good friend to Beth and Christie and the rest, a nice sister to your bossy brothers, a loyal supporter of the Smurfs, and a close follower of Jesus.

I hope your next year is even happier than the ones you have known so far. Mom and I will do everything to make sure it is, not just with money and clothes and toys, but also with prayers and advice and hugs.

Happy birthday, Carrie.

I go before you always

If there's one spiritual idea I would like to leave with my children, it is a notion of God's love for them—a love which keeps him ever near them, always involved with them, and constantly ready to help them.

At some time in their lives, they will feel that God is absent. That's understandable. A worse feeling, however, is that God is around but not really too interested in them. An apathetic

God is worse than an absent one.

When our oldest, Jimmy, was making his college choice, I suggested that he ask God's advice.

"God doesn't care what college I go to," he protested.

"Sure he does," I insisted. "He wants the best for you. He wants you to become smarter, to make the right career decision. He cares."

"He's got too much to worry about," Jimmy said. "Too many important things, like nuclear war and cancer."

"What if you're the guy who's going to prevent that war or cure cancer?" I replied.

"Sure, Dad," he answered.

"God cares about you," I repeated. "He watches over you. Like when you drive and don't get in an accident."

"What do you think—that he controls the steering wheel?"

"No, you do," I said. "But he cares if you're reckless. He wants you to drive safely. And if you're hurt by someone else, he'll be there to comfort you and us and the other people."

"Do you think he's going to announce a college to me?"

"He'll talk to you, but in different ways," I said. "Through me and your mom, through your friends, through your counselor, through the catalogs that appeal to you. Ask him to be involved."

I don't know what Jimmy did, but I hope some part of the message got through.

Next time, I'll set my alarm

Our son Jimmy, 19, came up with a great one-liner during a recent discussion of differences in dating styles. Mary and I

Finding God in Your House

asked him why he didn't follow his girlfriend, Christine, home when she left our house at 2 a.m., long after we had gone to sleep.

"I used to do that when I was dating your mother," I told Jimmy, who responded with a look that said, "Yeah, and they used to have coal chutes and buttonhooks, too."

"She lives out in the sticks," Mary lectured. "What if her car broke down?"

Jimmy shrugged. The shrug said, "Cars don't have cranks anymore, and they invented Triple-A."

"I think you should have followed her," I said.

Mary nodded. "Your father would have done it."

"Then," said Jimmy, "I should have woke him up!"

CHAPTER 4

Conversing with Carrie

God is great, God is good

I like to let conversations about religion come out of natural situations and unguarded moments. If I announced, "It's time to discuss theology," my family would flee. Justifiably. So I try to sneak it in. Over the years, through this method, I've had some enlightening talks with my daughter, Carrie. Enlightening for both of us.

Like the other day when Carrie was playing in the yard. It was a beautiful day and seemed like a great occasion to discuss how good God is. So I began the following dialogue, hoping it would educate without her being aware of it. Here's how the talk went:

Me: Carrie, what's the greatest thing about God?

Carrie: He made the whole world.

Me: What's the weirdest thing about him?

Carrie: He wasn't born.

Me (starting to worry; I hoped she wouldn't get too complicated for me): But Jesus was born.

Carrie: God wasn't.

Me: Right, but Jesus is God.

Carrie: He's his son.

Me: Right. So he's also God. (She wasn't buying this, so

Finding God in Your House

I moved on.) What's the best thing God ever made? (I was trying to outguess her. Would she say "the world" or "cartoons" or "orange popsicles"?)

Carrie: Me.

I didn't think she was that smart. It wasn't an egotistical thing she said—I'm pleased she feels that good about herself. Her parents, her brothers, her grandparents, her teachers in both Catholic school and religious education classes, and God can share the credit.

The easiest questions are the hardest to answer

Remember the joke about the child who asked his parents where he came from? The parents launched into a lengthy sex-education course and concluded by asking, "Does that answer your question?"

The boy shook his head. "Not really. My friend Bobby is from Cleveland. Where am I from?"

Parents can sometimes overload their kids or assume depth where there is only a mini-brain. Consider the following conversation between me and Carrie when she was in the first grade:

Carrie: Did Jesus die in the Holy Spirit?

Me (in my head): What does she mean? Is she referring to the charismatic experience of being indwelled by the third person of the Trinity? How does she know about that? I don't even understand it. Did the Spirit come on Jesus before the Pentecost? Let's see; the Spirit was there at his Baptism so. . . .

Carrie: Well?

Me (aloud): I would say that when Jesus died the Holy Spirit was within him and—

Carrie: No, no. Did he die in the Holy Spirit?

Me: Huh?

Carrie (gesturing): Up there.

Me (a light going on): You mean at our church? Holy Spirit parish?

Carrie: Yeah. Some people die in a car. Did he die in the Holy Spirit church?

Me: No.

I followed up with a brief geography lesson, but it was a natural question from someone who sees a crucifix in church, who hears about Jesus' death at every Mass, and who once asked about the pastor, "Is he God?"

That one was easier to answer.

Matthew, Mark . . . Impolians?

I forget the cause, but Carrie informed me that she could name all of Jesus' disciples.

"All twelve?" I asked.

She nodded and began:

"John . . . Mark . . . Paul. . . ."

She hesitated and pondered. I smiled an encouraging smile.

"Matthew," she continued.

"And?"

She squinted. "Did I say Paul?"

"Yes," I said, "Go on."

"Ah, Luther . . . Romans . . . and Impolians."

"Who?"

"Impolians," she affirmed. "It's spelled something like this: I-N-D-I-N-P-O-L-E-S."

64

"Impolians," I repeated.

"Yes," she said again.

She was short of her twelve, but I think she had gone far enough. Does anyone know who Impolians was?

Family humor should be a laughing matter

Carrie and I had another one of our wacky conversations the other day. A wacky conversation, in my view, is one in which she bests me in some category, such as humor, logic and how we see the world. She combined all three as we listened recently to a weather report on the radio. The weather forecaster was noting all the day's statistics, including high temperature, humidity and wind velocities. Then he came to the time the sun would set the next day. That began our little play:

Carrie: Who cares when the sun sets?

Me (summoning my "superior" wisdom to demonstrate how her worldview was limited): Owls—so they know when to start flying.

Carrie (with her patented sigh): Yeah, but they don't listen to the radio!

Ready for a hearty spring?

In spring a young man's fancy turns . . . and sometimes looks at my daughter. At the tender age of 9, Carrie is beginning to sense signs of deep and true love coming her way. At least, she thinks so. Here's a conversation we had:

Carrie: I think Jason is in love with me.

Me: Why?

Carrie: He smiles at me all the time.

Me: What else?

Carrie: The other day at school, he asked me if he should wear his coat when we went out to the playground.

Me: That means he's in love with you?

Carrie (exasperated at the questioning): Dad, he's even asking me what to wear now!

I guess that is a sign of love. I know that I always ask my wife what to wear when we go out. With friends, not to the playground.

I swear I wouldn't tell a soul

My children are getting wise to how often their comments and actions turn up in my writing. Carrie, who is 10, is especially wary. Recently, when she was having trouble coming up with the courage to stay overnight at friends' houses, I asked her what was bothering her. She eyed me suspiciously and went to the bookshelf. Pulling out a volume about saints, she marched back to me.

"Put your right hand on this," she commanded, "and swear you won't tell about this."

So I did, and I won't. But I didn't swear not to tell you about her making me swear.

Where's your umbrella, Gene Kelly?

The whole family was watching "That's Entertainment" on TV. You remember that movie; it's a compendium of famous scenes from movie musicals. One of the high points occurs when Gene Kelly dances through the water while "Singin' in the Rain."

Carrie observed silently for a while as he splashed about amid a torrent from the sky. Finally, when he doused his head beneath the water coursing off a drainpipe, she observed: "He must be sick."

Then she allowed just the right amount of silence before adding, "He will be in the morning."

Nice gift?

When Carrie was 6, she was invited to visit at a friend's house while the friend's older sister had a birthday party. It was decided that Carrie should take along a little gift. My wife Mary purchased it and wrapped it up before Carrie saw it.

"It's a book. A diary," her mother informed her as she sent her on her way.

Later, the friend's mother called to tell us that Carrie had presented the gift with little ceremony. "You didn't have to get something," she was told.

"It's nothing," Carrie replied. "Just a diarrhea book."

I believe the expression is, "We have a little communications problem."

CHAPTER 5

Midlife goes on

The good young days

Maybe it's turning 40 that did it, but I've spent an awful lot of time lately thinking about my youth. The smallest memory can turn me blurry-eyed with nostalgia; some small sense experience—a chilly morning, the smell of bacon—will almost literally transport me back to my childhood.

Getting an invitation to the 25th anniversary of my grade-school graduating class didn't help. With the invitation came a list of school memories like air-raid drills, yellow ocher and glazed donuts. They mean nothing to you, of course; but they instantly stir in me thoughts of St. Ann's School—the girls with SAS on their plaid uniforms, the boys in the schoolyard passing a football and my living close enough to go home for lunch.

That walk to and from school is something I focus on often, not only as my route for eight years, but also as the path I walked at 6 a.m. on winter mornings to serve Mass. I can still see the darkness, feel the cold snap of air, hear the snow crunch.

I remember the first Mass I served. The night before, my parents informed me they would not be getting up that early to go to Mass. They wished me well, making sure that I knew all the Latin words from *Introibo ad altare* to the closing prayers at the foot of the altar.

Finding God in Your House

I made the lonely trek the next morning, feeling somewhat abandoned. Things brightened considerably when the older server permitted me to light the candles and then take the position which would allow me to ring the bells. I still appreciate this unexpected display of generosity from an old hand at serving.

With our backs to the people, the priest and we altar boys went through the ritual until Communion; I accompanied the celebrant to the rail with my paten. (How many clues to the era are in that sentence?)

Among the first people I came to were my parents. They had been there all along, watching me without making me nervous. It felt good to see them.

This nostalgia itch got so bad recently that I called Hartland, Wisconsin. That's bad because I have never been there. But that town was the site of the manufacturer of some toys I have clung to ever since grade school. They are plastic figures of the then-popular TV cowboys, like the Lone Ranger and Bret Maverick. (Come on, admit it; I've got you nostalgic now, too, right?) I wanted to find out if these souvenirs of boyhood were worth anything monetarily; I already knew they had incalculable value as talismans of the past.

You can't go home again, the man said, and I should have remembered that. The toys of my youth, manufactured in the aptly-named "Hartland," were no longer being made; and the company had been bought out and was now part of Plastech Research. A novelist couldn't have chosen better names to indicate the changes in society over the last three decades.

So be careful when you pursue your memories. Sometimes you can come up against something called Plastech.

James Breig

As I watch my children now from that secret vantage point of age which parents occupy, I wonder what their memories will be. What toys, which events, which friends will cause them to mist over when they reach the supposed halfway point of life? And will I be among those memories?

Tame the mid-life crisis

As I turn the corner on 40 and head toward 41, I become more and more aware of my age. I haven't spent this much time thinking about how old I am since I was turning 10—getting in double numbers, you know. Even turning 30 didn't cause me to spend so much time reflecting on where I've been and what I still want to do.

Are these the signs pointing the way to the cliff labeled mid-life crisis? If so, people keep mailing me new reasons to jump right over. First, my mother, going through the drawers, closets and trunks that make her home a repository of our past, sent me a postcard she found. It was first sent in the summer of 1952 when I was between kindergarten and first grade. It came from my brother Joe, six years my senior, who was away at Boy Scout camp.

In his scrawly handwriting (his penmanship is the same today), he informed me that he "just went on an overnight canoe hike like the Indians used to do." The front of the postcard was typed on the same typewriter my mother still uses. It is obvious that she had pre-addressed the card so Joe would write me.

Of course, I have no memory of the card or the canoe trip or that summer. But now, like something an archaeologist has

Finding God in Your House

uncovered, comes this artifact of my childhood, flooding my mind with images of crew cuts, lead soldiers, drinking the milk from some weed that grew in our front yard (what was that stuff anyway?), and feeling sad when Ed Sullivan was on because it meant the next day was the start of another school week.

Fade out on the first grader. Fade in on the freshman. I recently received the alumni newsletter from my high school. I turned to the section that covered the year I graduated. There, peering out at me, was a photo of a classmate named Tony. I just stared at it. It looked like a trick. Like someone had taken Tony's yearbook picture and painted his temples gray, darkened the skin under his eyes, and paled his face a little. He looked, in fact, like a sophomore made up as an old man for the school play.

What happened to you, Tony? More importantly, what happened to me? Where did the years go? Where did our dark hair, bright eyes and flushed skin go?

I like a lot of things about being 40. The maturity, the confidence, the experience, the beginnings of wisdom (maybe, just around the edges). But you can have the midnight weariness, the bald spot, and the sense that, somehow, two decades between college and now were stolen overnight.

The other day my wife, Mary, and I attended a ceremony at our oldest son's high school. Jimmy, now 17, stood in front with his classmates; and I was time-tunneled back through the '80s, the '70s, and the '60s. Suddenly, I saw myself standing there with the hopeful (and somewhat confused) look of a teenager on the brink of tomorrow. I also saw my brother in Jimmy's features. Mary sees her father in his leanness, the long nose, the jawline. But I see Joe, who was always skinner than me

71

(the rat), and who always stood with that same posture that Jimmy has.

Watching him gave me mixed feelings. I felt proud of him while I mused about time's flight. I felt nostalgic for the days when I was the student taking part in the rites of passage, but I also felt relieved to know that I would never again experience love's rejection or a C-minus or the other thumps that batter the late teens. I longed for the vigor and newness of being 17, but I also welcomed the sureness and stability of 40.

Then I suddenly and unexpectedly realized, with a shudder, that I have been driving for almost a quarter century. Odd thoughts that group strange sections of time become more and more prevalent I've found lately. It's a good way to drive yourself crazy. (Let's see: I remember when Kennedy died, but people now in college think of Dallas only as a TV series.)

If I'm lucky, I've lived half my life. I pray that the second half will be better than the first. But, on the whole, I don't have any kicks coming about that portion. Still, if people could stop sending me signals from the past, I would be able to get on with 41.

The trouble is, I bet, those signals most often originate somewhere inside me, bells that remind me life cannot be lived without telephone lines connecting people to everything that came before.

Lately, those phones have been ringing a lot.

My sweater, my friend

I have managed to hang on to the sweater, but the Hawaiian shirt got kidnapped and is gone forever.

Finding God in Your House

The shirt came to me years ago from an uncle I never knew I had until just before he died. My mother's half-brother, he had disappeared into the West, lost contact with the family and had rarely been spoken about. Then, one day when I was in high school, mom told me that Uncle Ralph was coming for a visit. Uncle Who? He turned out to be a nice guy whose one visit was pleasant. When he died shortly after, his effects ended up at our house. Among them was a pile of loud shirts, short-sleeved, of course, because of the California heat. I selected one of them as a keepsake.

That shirt moved with me when I got married and became my mowing-the-lawn shirt. I loved it. I could sweat into it, get it grass-stained and wipe motor oil on it. It didn't matter what I did to it. It was loyal, familiar and always there. Like an old setter. When I donned it, I meant business: The grass was going to be cut, by gum.

Then came the day it got kidnaped. My heartbeat picked up its pace. My palms sweated. I couldn't find The Shirt. I went through my closet from left to right and back again, paging past other shirts and suits and sweaters. No Hawaiian shirt. The kidnapper was not difficult to guess.

"Where's my grass-cutting shirt?" I asked my wife Mary.

"Hmm?" she replied offhandedly, hoping I would find something else to do besides grill the guilty party.

"What did you do with it?"

She got that look that wives get when they have mixed up their husband's baseball card collection, thrown out the latest issue of Sports Illustrated or drunk the last Pepsi. "Oh, did you want that old thing? It was so ratty. I threw it away."

A spring cleaning fit had killed my shirt. My shoulders

slumped. I wanted to scream: "Threw it away? Would you toss our kids into the trash? That shirt had history written all over it in stains. That's like selling the Shroud of Turin at a garage sale!" That shirt was precious. That shirt was Uncle Ralph's. Did her treachery have any bounds?

When I asked that question of myself, my mouth went dry. She wouldn't have killed two pieces of clothing, would she? I raced back to the closet and shuffled through the shirts, suits and—ah! there it was. My black sweater with the white piping. The one which came from the manufacturer with six buttons but now has only the bottom one. The sweater I can wipe my hands on when I'm eating peanuts, the sweater which keeps me physically warm in the winter and emotionally warm when I'm sick, the sweater which I've worn over T-shirts in the summer in order to look a little more "presentable" when the doorbell rings. Mary had missed it during her cleaning binge.

I hugged my sweater. Although I no longer remember where it came from, I know that I need it like Linus needs his blanket. It feels good; it hugs me back; it doesn't mind if I toss it into a corner. Everyone laughs at us two, but we don't care. We have each other.

Things like my Hawaiian shirt and my black sweater connect me to the past. They tie me to distant places and events and people. They have to be kept, regardless of how they look, because they remind me that I am a creature of time who has memories of years ago as well as dreams for years to come.

Women have such things, too: old bathrobes, their wedding dresses, the thimbles their grandmas gave them, quilts. Men wouldn't think of throwing such things away because men know their value. Why is it, then, that a woman doesn't hesitate to

Finding God in Your House

toss out her husbands' baseball glove from Little League or the hubcaps from his dad's Rambler or the Hawaiian shirt from California that came from the Uncle Ralph he never knew he had?

Men sometimes get the bum rap that they don't have any sentimentality and feelings. They have them, but they're expected to smile and shrug anyway when they get put out with the trash.

On the air

Soon, I'll rustle around in the closet by the garage door and drag out an old reel-to-reel tape recorder that I bought with my first paycheck when I worked one summer in high school.

As I begin to set it up, my wife will roll her eyes and the older boys will say, "Not this again, Dad." Carrie will be my only supporter because she's still ham enough to eagerly participate in the show.

When I've finally got the tapes prepared and hooked up the microphone, I'll gather everyone in the room and sonorously intone into the machine with my best Dan Rather voice: "It's a chilly day. We had meat loaf for dinner. . . ."

Thus will begin another installment of our chronicles. For about twenty minutes, I will interview the children about their schoolwork, their favorite TV shows, their best friend, and their ambitions. They'll chat about who's in the World Series and tell jokes. Carrie, inevitably, will sing a song. Finally, I will cajole Mary into delivering an assessment of the growth and development of each child.

Then I'll sign off, rewind the tape and put the bulky machine back into the closet until next year.

75

James Breig

We now have a collection of audio tapes reaching back to when Jimmy, now nearly 17, was in first grade. The tapes tell of times before Carrie existed, when we lived in another house, when Gerald Ford was president, and when then-high-voiced Matt, now almost driving age, couldn't pronounce his kindergarten teacher's name.

It's a pain to do sometimes, but it's usually fun once we get going. And I know that someday, when they are all gone, and Mary and I swing on the porch at the old folks' home, the tapes will be precious reminders of the way we were.

We'll recall when we bought the carpeting for upstairs, when my father died, when Carrie's career dream was to be "a radio-clock manager" (whatever that is), how Jimmy and Emmett remained friends from first grade through college and beyond, how Matt's schoolwork proceeded, who was dating whom, and what we made of it all.

It would be much easier to begin it now, what with cassette recorders with built-in mikes. Wealthier folks can even add video to the process. Whatever, I'd encourage you to begin now to build your own library of memories. It doesn't matter how old your kids are or even if you've got any. Just do it so when gray-and-wrinkle time arrives, you'll have something to hang onto.

Child's art improves with age

Hold on to your past.

Don't throw out those old toys and drawings from first grade; your kids will want them someday. Make a family tree before you forget who your great-grandmother was. And find ways to get the older folks in your family to recall the past so you can pass it on.

I was reminded of this when I received a letter from my older sister, who has fourteen years on me. In it, she mentioned Victor Borge, the pianist-comedian who is our mother's favorite.

"I first saw him," my sister writes, "with Mom when she was pregnant with you. We laughed so hard we thought sure she was going to give birth right then and there."

That's a story I had never heard before, and it means nothing to you (and probably little to my sister and mother). But it means a lot to me because it places me in my family at the earliest date possible. Some fascinating questions arise: Was Victor Borge's the first voice I heard prenatally? How close did I come to being born in an auditorium? How much of my sense of humor derives from my mother, who, when she gets going, can laugh longer and harder than anyone else I know?

As I say, you don't care. But someone in your family has a story about you that you would care about if you knew it. Start asking around. Who knows what tales might surface about your nine months inside your mom.

Treasures keep the past at hand

I know how to get my mother angry in one easy step. In fact, it's the only way that was guaranteed to get her peeved at me. So, of course, I made sure to pull her chain whenever we were together.

All I had to do was to say: "Baseball cards."

This usually elicited a motherly "Oh, shut up" from her.

James Breig

She knew I was teasing, and I know she was only a little bit miffed; but, gosh, I wish she hadn't given away my collection of baseball cards.

The worst thing about it is not that the collection probably contained one of those expensive Mickey Mantle cards, but that it is the only thing my mother ever threw away. She made a pack rat look profligate. At one point in her life she collected beds, storing them in the attic and basement for occasions when guests called and sleeping arrangements had to be juggled to make our home into a hostelry that rivaled Hilton's. But in various drawers, closets and cupboards of her home, she also put away all sorts of memorabilia smaller than twin beds.

Except for my baseball cards. When my family visits the old homestead, my children can play with toys I used 30 years ago. They'll find the Hardy Boys and Lone Ranger books my older brother read. And my daughter can dress dollies my sisters cradled in the '40s and '50s.

But they won't find the sweet-smelling pieces of cardboard adorned with the likes of Walt Dropo, Sad Sam Jones, The Klu, Jim Konstanty and Jim Gentile. Those my mother gave away to the little boy next door without even asking me. A boy who knew nothing about Rocky Colavito, Sal Maglie and Preacher Roe.

I miss those cards, but I like to find other objects from my childhood, like old report cards, class photos from the days of crew cuts, and lead soldiers. That's why I keep a little spot in one desk drawer at home where I toss things which, when they surface from the past someday may please my children. I put in drawings and letters and pictures and even calendars on which my wife has marked all the days of their lives, and the appointments which are so mundane now but will one day become quaint, nostalgic and warm remembrances of the past.

The archaeology of family life is too easily lost. We live in a throw-away society where today's toys become passé tomorrow and nothing is made to last past the weekend. I think my kids will someday appreciate the fact that I kept some of their childhood stored in boxes and drawers and closets. A baseball cap here, a kindergarten artwork there, an old water pistol or a rock collection that's only a closet shelf away. The handling of these in decades to come will link the children to their past, the family, my wife and me. And, when their children ask, "What's this funny-looking thing?" or "Did you really play with something as silly as that?" they, too, will be tied into us.

I invite you to find a cubbyhole somewhere in your home where you can store away memories in the guise of discarded teddy bears or primitive clay sculptures. Someday, you'll be happy you bothered.

Every now and then, my sons drag me to a baseball-card show where merchants display rectangular relics of my past. I linger now and then over a photo a Gil McDougald or the Topps series which was printed to look like images on a TV set. But I don't buy. Those cards, after all, weren't mine and you can't purchase the past; you can only save it.

A head of the game?

To get this joke, you have to know that I have a bald spot on the back of my head (a teeny-weeny one, honest—well, okay, it's the size of a pancake). I also have a crown, that is, a fake tooth. And, recently, to complete this homely portrait, my face broke out for reasons I still don't comprehend.

Pretty picture, huh?

So my son Matt looked me over one day and said, "Gee, you're losing your teeth and getting zits. If this is your second childhood, maybe you'll grow hair again."

CHAPTER 6

Block those stereotypes

More work to do

I guess I have to return the award. At least, I'd better do some
quick educating in order to keep it. I refer to an award I received
from a local council of churches for my efforts on behalf of
ecumenism. When I returned home with it, Carrie, our 8-year-
old, asked who gave it to me.

"Some Christians," I replied.

"I ain't no Christian," she said. "I'm a Catholic."

Let's see . . . in seven words, my daughter managed to insult everyone who isn't a Catholic by implying that she wouldn't
want to be one and to insult every Catholic by implying that
they are not Christians. That about covers it, I guess.

On another occasion, Carrie and I carried on an interfaith
discussion. We were about to watch an episode of "Highway
to Heaven" and the previews made it clear that the show was
going to deal with the Holocaust. So, while the commercials
ran, I shut off the sound and said to her, "Do you know who
the Jews are?"

"Sure," she replied. "They're just people."

I should have stopped there, but of course, I blundered on.
"Right," I replied. "And what kind of people?"

She pulled her thumb out of her mouth long enough to say,

"They don't go to church, they don't pray, and they don't believe in God."

Yipes! my mind said; no wonder they keep doing programs about the Holocaust. So we talked about who the Jews really are and began listing some famous Jews, including Jesus, his parents, all the apostles, Moses, Albert Einstein, Beverly Sills, Woody Allen, and the star of "Highway to Heaven."

Then Carrie recalled that, indeed, she has a classmate who is "half-Jewish and half-Catholic." I suggested that her friend probably prayed, believed in God, and went to some place of worship on the weekend.

She seemed content with our discussion, but I wonder where she got her initial impression. My fear is that the Gospels or her religious education classes still give her the idea that it was the Jews who were responsible for Christ's death or for at least ignoring his message, thus giving Jews the image Christ first had.

We blame TV for a lot of screwy ideas which kids come up with, but I suspect, in this case, the blame lay elsewhere.

Pretty in pink

The first time I became aware that children are colorblind when it comes to race occurred when my two sons were in grade school. My wife, Mary, and I were sitting at the kitchen table with them, talking about a major addition to the household: Mary was pregnant with our third child. The boys were discussing their future sibling and what he or she would look like.

"Is it a boy or a girl?" one of them wondered.

"We don't know," Mary replied.

"What color will it be?" Jimmy asked.

Finding God in Your House

Astonished, I said, "What color do you think?"

"Maybe white," Matt answered. "Maybe black."

"Why would it be black?" Mary asked.

"Why not?" Jimmy said. "Some of the Layman kids are white . . ."

". . . and some are black," Matt finished. "So what color will the new baby be?"

Mary and I exchanged a look of wonder and began to laugh. The Laymans are one of those unique couples who have compiled a family by adopting a mixed brood of kids, one of whom, indeed, was black. To Jimmy and Matt, their family was no different from ours; so why shouldn't our newest come out Chinese or Mexican?

Mary and I then delivered a quick lesson in genetics, adoption and the guaranteed whiteness of our newest, but I was left with a warm sense of how nice children can be. Kids judge others on bases which make sense ("Timmy is a jerk," they will say, not because Timmy is white or black or handicapped or anything else exterior; he's a jerk because of his behavior).

I wonder how much my sons learned from my lecture on Mendel and how much they gleaned from our reaction. Our words were probably clumsy and slightly incoherent as Mary and I searched our memories for information stored there from high-school biology classes. Clearer, no doubt, was our surprise, worn on our faces like exclamation points. We weren't being racist in our facial response; we didn't grimace or make a "yecch" sound at their suggestion that the newborn could be black or brown. But we did communicate the idea that it would be odd to be a skin shade that isn't "our color."

There are lots of ways of teaching that there's something privileged about being pink. White parents don't have to sit around cussing Martin Luther King to convey their feelings; they can also do it by more subtle and sometimes even unconscious methods, like making a face when walking past a Hispanic person or mumbling something about it "getting awful dark out" when driving through a predominantly black neighborhood. Even well-intentioned parents who struggle to live a life free of racism can be caught in traps when cliches ("lazy Mexicans") and jokes ("Hear the one about the five black guys?") come out of mouths unguarded by brains.

That child-to-be who prompted these thoughts turned out to be a girl (white, as promised). Nine years later, I've witnessed Carrie's color blindness. When she describes children at her school, it is never in terms of their color. For instance, it was only when one of her friends turned up for a birthday party that I discovered she had a white mother and a black father. Of course, since I am worldly-wise, I always imagine her friends as white. Did my daughter catch another look of surprise on my face and, if so, what did she learn from that echo of the past?

Meanwhile, I've seen my innocent sons grow into a world where jokes about blacks, stereotyping them as basketball-playing idiots, get told around the same kitchen table where they once asked about their sister's hue. On such occasions, I put on my fatherly face to lecture about racism; inside, I am wondering what went wrong between childhood's innocence and adolescence.

The song from "South Pacific" explains to children that "you've got to be taught to hate and fear; it's got to be drummed in your dear little ear," and that "you've got to be taught before it's too late to hate all the people your relatives hate." Original

Finding God in Your House

sin's power over children can be seen early in several areas, such as lying, stealing and the tendency to bop your playmates when they grab your toys. But racism seems to be something which requires lessons; it doesn't come with the umbilical cord.

The other day, I listened as Carrie's friend ridiculed some mentally handicapped children who were being "mainstreamed" at their school. "They smell," her friend declared knowingly, "and they try to hug you."

That night, as I tucked her in, I spoke to Carrie about her friend's remarks and about how we are to treat God's children, regardless of their condition.

As I lay in bed later on, I asked myself why we parents do it to our children. I spoke to myself about what a fine job adults are doing when it comes to teaching our kids the finer points of racism and xenophobia. They come into the world with no idea that black people have rhythm, that Jews love money, that Arabs stab you in the back, or that Puerto Ricans are lazy. They've "got to be taught," and some adults seem to be handing out master's degrees.

Still, there is cause for hope. Young blacks aren't being hanged in southern towns; Hispanics and Vietnamese are being welcomed into society with less animosity than greeted the Irish and Germans in the early part of this century; laws now protect those whom laws once persecuted.

As I dream about the future, I imagine my sons and daughter answering my grandchildren's questions, and I cherish a small wish that their responses will show that my lessons of voice and face and attitude helped make things better.

(Reprinted from *Salt* magazine, 205 West Monroe Street, Chicago, Illinois 60606).

James Breig

Feminine face for God

Have you talked to your children about God the Mother yet?
How about God the Cook?
God the Old Lady?

Sister Sandra Schneiders, associate professor of New Testament studies at Graduate Theological Union in Berkeley, California, believes it is "absolutely essential that we restore the feminine to God."

Notice that she said "restore." She isn't trying to create a new image of God, she explains; she merely is trying to reclaim images which have been ignored.

Of course, God, being spiritual, is neither male nor female; but the usual Christian approach is to refer to God as a father, as Jesus did, and to use masculine pronouns. But Schneiders wonders why people do not pay attention to those times Old Testament writers and Jesus referred to God as a woman.

"Most people are very surprised to learn that the metaphor of God as father is used very, very few times in the Old Testament," she noted during a recent lecture. On the other hand, Moses called God a mother in the Book of Numbers (11:12) while other references did the same (see Hosea and Isaiah 49).

As for Jesus, she said that he referred to God with female imagery. "In Luke 15, we have two parables," she said. "One is about a shepherd who lost a sheep. The other is about a woman who lost a coin. It's very interesting what happens to that metaphor. How many school children would guess that the woman who lost the coin is God? They all know that the shepherd who lost his sheep is God."

She also pointed to Matthew 13, in which Jesus used the parable of the baker-woman who "kneaded yeast into the dough

86

until the whole loaf was softened." The lesson is the same as the one found in the parable of the sower who reaped many times what he sowed.

"Why is it that we know the sower of the seed is God, but we don't realize that the baker-woman is God?" she asks.

Your kids will know it if you tell them the next time those parables come up in the Gospel, or during religious education classes or even just chatting around the dinner table.

The last thing your child needs is to be stereotyped

Parents like to issue rules, commandments and warnings to their children; these regulations usually begin with: "Thou shalt not." Since turnabout is fair play, here are some "don'ts" for moms and dads concerning how they raise their children:

• Don't stereotype your children according to their gender. It's our daughter, Carrie, who has shown the most interest in being an astronaut; it's our son Jim who would make a good teacher. If Sarah wants to learn household repairs while Bobby tinkers in the kitchen, let her. Women can be plumbers, too, and most of the famous chefs in the world are men.

Even more important than careers are emotions and spirituality. Don't lock your children into the belief that girls cry while boys tough it out or that women pray in church while men have a smoke out back.

Showing your children that their gender does not lock them away from feelings and futures is an important task for parents and one that begins from the first moments of life.

• Don't criticize your children all the time. Often, the only contact between parents and kids occurs when the former catches the latter doing something wrong and yells about it. Catch your children doing something right and tell them how proud you are of them. If your son's room is messy, say so; don't say, "You're a mess," or "You'll never listen to me." A good method of criticizing has been called "the Oreo method" of sandwiching a criticism between two compliments.

• Don't label your youngsters. Parents do this all the time: Kenny is "the smart one," Beulah is "the bookworm," Audrey is "our little angel," Hank is "the funny one." When that happens, children try to live up to the labels and lose the chance to explore other parts of their personalities. What's worse is when parents use negative labels: "He's our lazy son," "she's the black sheep," "the twins are difficult kids."

The same thing happens outside of families. I've heard actresses complain about being labeled as "blonde comediennes" incapable of dramatic roles; companies issue press releases to make sure their product isn't pigeon-holed into one niche in the market. Labels fence people in; parents should be gate builders.

• Don't have all the teaching about faith in your family come from one parent, namely the mother. Telling children about God, prayer, the Mass, spirituality, the saints and so on is men's work, too. As a result of previous generations' ignoring my first "don't" about gender stereotyping, many fathers think that only women are capable of teaching about faith, and that somehow it isn't manly to explain to kids how much God loves them.

There are all sorts of advantages to putting up "men at work" signs when it comes to telling children about faith, one of them affects men themselves. Writing in *U.S. Catholic* magazine, Kenneth Guentert notes: "Teaching religion changed my life. It showed me something I didn't know—that I could enjoy children. It demanded skills I didn't know I had and enabled me to discover my own inner child.'' Ken was writing about formal teaching and being a religious education instructor, but his words apply also to dads.

• Don't compare your children to each other. Doing so creates a sibling rivalry that can last a lifetime. I remember following my brother, who was six years older, into schools and being asked why I couldn't play basketball as well as he did. Other children get asked why they aren't as smart or as pretty or as outgoing as a sister who preceded them. That same comparing happens within families. Have you ever heard yourself saying things like these to one of your children: "Why can't you keep your room as clean as your sister does?" or "Your brother always gets his schoolwork done on time; what's wrong with you?" or "Your sister doesn't talk back like that"?

Anna Quindlen, a columnist for *The New York Times,* recently wrote about how hard she tries to avoid comparing her children: "It is not fair to make two children foils for one another, although it is common and, I suppose, understandable to do so. It can also turn to poison faster than you can say Cain and Abel. . . . The danger in making our children take roles on opposite sides of the family room is that the contradictions in their own characters, the things that make humans so interesting, get flattened out and hidden away. The other danger is that they will hate one another.''

So knock it off. Now!

Stereotypes can go both ways

A friend told me this story about how television can offer some fairly odd stereotypes to go with the usual ones:

James Breig

"My daughter, who's in kindergarten, was watching TV with me one night. I forgot what show it was, but it involved a man who was acting like he was drunk. She turned to me and asked, 'Can women get drunk?'

"It was a fairly strange question until I thought about it. When TV or films show someone drunk, it's most likely a man—whether the plot is a comedy sketch or a drama. Beer commercials focus primarily on men, showing them hoisting a few cans after working in a blast furnace.

"What made her question all the more interesting is that her grandmother is an alcoholic. My daughter probably doesn't recognize this and has not really seen her grandma in an obviously tipsy condition—the sort of staggering, stuttering cliché of the comedy drunk.

"So I explained to her that anyone can get drunk and that alcohol can be very damaging. But so can stereotypes. Feminists rightly complain about negative images of their sex; maybe men should do the same when they are presented as the only ones who can get drunk."

Attention, K-Mart shoppers

I was standing recently just inside the doors of the K-Mart near my home waiting for a ride to arrive. A black woman stood outside the doors collecting money for a charity. As shoppers exited, she would hold out her coffee can, bid them good day, and smile.

The scene soon became a lesson in sociology for me.

First I noticed how many ways people can evade someone who is asking for money. I've done it myself. You try to leave

Finding God in Your House

through the door farthest from the solicitor. Or you try to time your departure for the moment when someone else has occupied the solicitor by stuffing a bill into the tin can.

A very popular method is to talk with someone while exiting in order to pretend you don't notice the volunteer. If you're alone, you try to mingle with a crowd so you won't be picked out for a smile, a hello and that look of hope.

Next I observed how color played a role. White people, for the most part, declined to give, while black people dropped a donation in the can. Did the white people automatically suspect a black person asking for money, or did they assume the charity was one of "theirs"? Do black people avoid white solicitors?

Then I began to realize the irony. Here were people who were, generally speaking, well-off. Sure, they were shopping at a discount store, but they were shopping. Not for bread and water but for waffle irons, candy, tires and shampoo. They had spendable income. They had just put down some bucks on something to make their lives more comfortable. And yet hardly anyone would cough up a buck for the woman with the tin can.

Why not? Because they give generously to other groups? I hope so. Or is it because they all have a streak of selfishness and saw no profit in giving away a dollar? After all, they were walking out of K-Mart with something in their hands. If they gave something to her, they would leave the parking lot with a little less in their pockets.

I pondered all this until my ride arrived.

I know. You wonder if I parted with a buck. Of course, I did. Otherwise, I wouldn't have been able to preach at you for the last few paragraphs.

CHAPTER 7

How the Good News handles bad news

What's up, Doc?

Here's how a recent period of "good news/bad news" went:

• Day 1: after two months of hurting every time she ate, one hospitalization, and several tests, my wife, Mary, found herself in even more intense pain.

Bad news: more tests led to her being hospitalized a second time.

• Day 2: a freak snowstorm (called "possible showers" the night before by weather forecasters) reduced several neighboring counties to official disaster areas and downed a record number of power lines, leaving us at home and Mary at the hospital in the dark.

• Day 3: with the power still out, the children had no school, but I had work. Bad news: the water had gone the route of the electricity.

• Day 4: the doctor ordered more tests on Mary, including procedures that should be classified as cruel and inhuman punishment. Searching for the cause of her pain, he was seeking evidence that it was her gall bladder. But blood tests, X rays, a CAT-scan, an upper GI series, an endoscopy, a hydascan (am I spelling these correctly?), and the mysterious ERCP showed nothing. ERCP stands for the complete name of the test, which even the doctor resisted pronouncing. It involves putting a tube down one's throat ("one" does not equal the doctor) and poking around looking for this and that. Mary's ERCP had proven neither negative nor positive; it was simply a failure because the two doctors who tried could not get the tube to go where they wanted it once it was in her stomach.

Being a worrier when the occasion warrants, I immediately began thinking of the worst possible things she could have.

Bad news: a second ERCP was ordered. The test, which is supposed to last 90 minutes, took four hours. At one point, in the middle of the exam, the electricity went out. At another point, the machine failed, leading to her being hoisted—tube in place—onto a stretcher and moved down a hall to another room for the continuation of the test.

Good news: they finally found some small indications that her problem was indeed her gall bladder, an organ you can live without. Doctors recommended surgery.

• Day 5: for the third day, the power remained out in hundreds of thousands of homes, including ours; but the hospital's had been restored. I told Mary she should be happy to be in a warm, lighted place. She offered to trade with me. I still resisted swapping.

Well, to make an already long story slightly shorter, Mary had her surgery.

So why tell you about this now that it's over? There are a couple of reasons. For one thing, I'd like to salute all our neighbors. Our closest relatives are 500 miles away, so it fell to friends, co-workers and neighbors to play the roles often assumed by siblings and parents. They brought in meals (once the power was restored), baby-sat Carrie, visited Mary (a work of mercy that is not emphasized enough; until I'd seen how much good it can do by watching Mary's reaction to visitors, I didn't realize how important it was to patients), and did a hundred tiny things that made life more bearable.

I also want to thank them and you for your prayers for Mary. Most of our friends are actively religious and always noted that they were praying for her. (One neighbor, who is not religious, said that "my fingers are crossed for her"; I appreciated his sincere concern, but it's not the same.)

As for your prayers, I hope you'll offer them now, retroactively, for Mary. Since God is not bound by time, you can petition him now for Mary's health and I already know that he has answered your prayers.

Sounds like "The Twilight Zone," doesn't it? It's not; it may be mysterious, but it's not weird. It's the communion of believers, a group that supersedes time and place.

So, thanks for the prayers that you're about to say; they worked.

My sister . . . I think I'll keep her

My sister is a chronological wonder. Geena is two years younger than I am but has the energy of someone half my age. She also has more endurance, patience and selflessness than I have. For the last eighteen months, she has been juggling three bowling balls with grace and style; they look as light as powder puffs when she tosses them about.

The first weight is our mother, who has been fighting cancer. Geena and her husband, Don, live with Mom. Geena takes her to the doctor, feeds her when Mom's interest flags, jollies her when Mom's spirits fade, and lies to the rest of the children about how serious the situation is. When I challenged her on that, she responded, "You've got your own problems. Why should you be depressed about this, too? I let you know enough."

Geena's husband is the second burden. He has been battling his own physical ailments, complicating her caregiving. He's missed a lot of work and needs comforting, too. He has his own schedule of doctor appointments and out-patient visits. But Geena copes, runs errands, keeps schedules straight, and includes Don in everything. He's amazing, too. Despite his own problems, he pitches in to help his mother-in-law.

The last bowling ball is Geena's job. Fortunately, it is not one that requires her to work 40 hours a week. She's been able to set her own hours for the most part. But it is one that requires a large emotional commitment: she tries to find foster and adoptive parents for hard-to-place children.

You'd think Geena would be a wreck. But listen to my 11-year-old daughter, Carrie, who wrote about her aunt for a school essay: "Geena has a voice like the soft summer breeze. Her hair is like soft, feathery clouds when a storm is brewing. Her cheeks are like two angels singing the Hallelujah chorus on Christmas Day. Geena is like a soft, cuddly, bouncy, lovable teddy bear."

How does she do it? What reserves does she draw from? What gives her encouragement to go on? I think she'd answer, in her typical style (and one that comes from our mom), "I just do it."

There are a lot of Geenas in the world, people who have given up their own careers and dreams to serve someone else. They are a selfless crew of saints-in-the-making who have surrendered their own needs to somebody else's. This article is my way of saying thanks to Geena for doing it.

One last example for a son

My sister's husband died as he wanted to: at home in his wife's arms.

Smitty had struggled against lung cancer for two years. I visited him for the last time a few weeks before his death. As I was leaving, pretending we'd see each other again, he took my hand and said, "Thanks for everything." I thought he meant for driving five hours to see him, so I brushed him off. "No," he said, correcting my impression, "I mean thanks for everything—from the beginning."

He was referring to the first years of his marriage when family troubles had come between him, his wife and my parents. I had tried—clumsily—to mediate, and he remembered my effort.

It was like him not to pretend at that last farewell. Smitty was a blunt man. After his funeral, his children joked about the commandments he had laid down for them with a sternness that would make Jehovah envious. I recalled that one of his most cogent responses to a counterargument was simply to repeat, "No, no, no," while he banged his fist into his other palm.

But Smitty was also a sensitive man. I never once spoke to him on the phone that he didn't ask me how my children were and what I was doing to show them the right way to live. He had an especially soft spot for my daughter, Carrie, who had once performed an impromptu song and dance for him. She had delighted him with her carefree performance, and he never forgot it.

Finding God in Your House

Most of all, Smitty was an heroic man who faced his final days with perseverance and without complaint. My sister, Betty, told me why he had been so strong: "He said, after the doctor told him he had only a short time to live, 'I guess I have one more thing I can do for my son. I can show him how a man dies.''

This man died on a Wednesday evening as his wife held him. His last sentence was, "Get people around you," a final Smittyesque command on how to behave. Betty did get people around her as friends and relatives jammed her home after the funeral and told stories about Smitty and hugged her.

"He wanted to show his son how to die," Betty told me. "I wanted to show our son what a marriage was, how a couple can help each other even in the worst times. I didn't lose a husband. I lost half of me."

At his funeral, we sang about how "amazing grace" saved a wretch like me. It also saved a man like Smitty.

The sound of tapping feet on heaven's highway

There are new sounds in heaven today: the sound of an 80-year-old woman's tap-dancing feet along the golden stairs . . . the sound of Fred Astaire and Bojangles gasping in admiration . . . the sound of two children laughing at their mother as she shuffles off to Buffalo . . . the sound of a husband applauding mightily.

My mother, Mary, always told us kids that, when she died and got to heaven (she never said "if") she would ask God for the ability to tap-dance. She had other requests, such as a logical explanation for mosquitoes. But, again and again, she

97

reiterated the playful wish for the power to make her feet move in wild control.

Less than an hour ago, I got word that Mom had died. Less than an hour ago, I'm sure, God began giving out tap shoes.

The laughing children watching her do a time-step are the brother and sister I never knew, children who died at birth and who now get to play with their mother. They will all make up for lost time where there is no time.

The clapping husband is my father. When he died several years ago, my mother was mad at him. "He always promised me," she said, "that I would die first and that he would carry me off to bury me in the backyard." To be buried in the yard she loved, among the flowers in which the two of them so often saw God, was an end she longed for, an end she was cheated of when he died first. I'll bet he still carried her off. But when he set her down, her feet began that rhythmic tapping she loved so much.

Sometimes, 80 years seems like a long time. Right now, it doesn't seem like my mother got enough time to enjoy the dances in between two world wars, a depression, the loss of her children and her final illness. But then I think of the good times she enjoyed, especially the good times she brought to others. Mom was one of those people who elevated hospitality to an art form. Scratch that cliché; she made it an act of sanctity. She raised five children, loved her husband, welcomed an endless stream of visitors and relatives who considered our home an inn, made neighbors and strangers feel instantly a part of the family, and then topped it all off by volunteering to run the parish religious education program at an age when everyone else thought about cutting back.

Finding God in Your House

If you want to understand my mother, read the New Testament—especially the parts about the Good Samaritan, about going the extra mile, about both Martha and Mary, and about the Beatitudes. Now you're close to knowing her.

For the past eighteen months, Mom had battled cancer as it spread from kidney to lung to brain. As she did, I increased my trips across the 500 miles that had separated us for the last eighteen years. In the hospital when her lung cancer was first diagnosed, as she struggled to breathe, I sat on the bed with her and rested her against my chest as I patted her.

"This is when I miss your father the most," she said between gasps. "I need someone to hold me when things go wrong and to tell me everything will be all right."

She said it again a year later when I brought her home from the hospital after a shunt had been put into her head to relieve the pressure from the tumor in her brain. Her head half shaved, exhausted from the surgery, wobbly from the effects of her disease, she tried to maneuver with a walker from the kitchen to her bed. Halfway there, she stalled.

"If I picked you up and carried you, would you be embarrassed?" I asked.

She let me know she didn't need me that much yet. She made it to the bed and slumped on the edge. Again, I sat beside her and cradled her and rubbed her back while I reflected on all the times she must have rocked me, hugged me, comforted me. Life isn't pretty all the time: she held my head when I vomited, she wiped my rear when I dirtied my diapers, she let me cry into her shoulder when I felt lost. On second thought, life is pretty at those times because love is beautiful. So I rocked her and patted her and tried to return the favors.

"This is when I miss your dad," she began.

On my last visit, she was unable to move her legs at all and had to be lifted from bed to chair and back again. Barely able to communicate, there were no spoken wishes for her husband, but the wishes were there nonetheless. One time, when I lifted her and held her against me while my wife changed her clothes, I asked playfully, "Do you want to dance?"

She laughed. It was one of the last sounds I heard from her. It was also, knowing her, probably one of the first sounds I heard from her. I'll bet, under that final laughter, she was saying inside, "Yes, I want to dance. I want to tap-dance."

Christa, Christ, and crisis: how to break bad news to kids

The aftershocks of the Challenger shuttle explosion lasted a long time. Shortly after the event that cost seven men and women their lives, I spoke with a child psychologist about how the disaster, witnessed by so many children, might affect little ones. She pointed out that there are no easy answers. Some children might be bothered immediately; some might not be bothered at all; others might delay their reaction for a while. For some, it could be a time of great difficulty and worry and fear—about their own parents' safety, for instance. For others, it could translate into personal concern.

I suspected that my daughter, Carrie, would display some signs of concern. At 8, she has shown a curiosity about death that began when my father died a few years ago and that I suspected would be intensified by the shuttle deaths.

For a time she was silent; then she began joking about the

100

tragedy, a classic way to handle sadness (how else do you account for the one-liners about Christa McAuliffe that surfaced within hours of the explosion?). Then she came up to me and said, as plainly as Dan Rather, "Are the solid-fuel rockets and the main booster radio-controlled?"

For her to use such technical language meant she had been paying close attention to the news. And that meant it was on her mind. So we talked about it.

When the shuttle went down, I realized for the first time what a disadvantage a public school can be on such occasions. Catholic schools could offer prayers and talk about the afterlife and discuss religious feelings about death. At her school, Carrie could hear only scientific explanations about the causes.

When Christa died, it was important to talk about Christ's death and Resurrection. We did that and her religious education classes did it—the twin backups to public education's necessary lack of religious instruction. The event brought home to me how significant family religious input is for those children who do not attend Catholic schools. Mary and I could be lazier about it when the two boys were in parochial school (although we were still not excused). With Carrie, though, we have to be more vigilant and diligent.

Carrie's ability to handle the next death in her life, private or public, has been strengthened, I believe. Death, after all, is a part of life.

How to face a funeral

A great deal of material has come my way about death: how to cope with it, how to explain it to children, how teens react to it, and so on. Here's a sampler for you to consider and apply to your own circumstances:

 • **On stillbirth**: "A baby's death, the loss of the baby that might have been, is experienced with an intense grief by the parents. A period of grieving is not only normal, it is necessary. The failure to go through the mourning process can lead to an unresolved grief, which may be expressed with physical illness or a severe depression"—Dr. Paula Adams Hillard, M.D., assistant professor of obstetrics and gynecology at the University of Cincinnati Medical Center, writing in *Parents* magazine.

My mother lost two children at birth, and I work with a woman who had the same experience with her first child. Since my wife, Mary, and I have never lost a child, I rely on their responses for an idea of how devastating that can be. I can imagine it, but their feelings show that my imagination cannot approach reality. They have carried the memory of those children with them since the day it happened.

Whenever they speak of those children, my mother and my co-worker grow misty-eyed and tight-throated even though it has been decades since they lost their babies.

Hillard, writing of a couple whose child had died in the womb, asked them if they would like to hold the baby when it was delivered. "When the stillborn baby boy was born, I wrapped him in a blanket," she recalls, "and April and Mark held him for about an hour. They told me that his name was James."

Holding the child if possible, naming him or her, being counseled by medical and chaplain staffs, and giving grief a chance are some of the steps Hillard recommends.

 • **Helping children understand**: when death invades children's lives, they need help in coping; and that help varies according to their ages. One way to help preschoolers is to deal with the subject before someone close to the child dies. The deaths of animals or unrelated people can lead children to ask about mortality, and parents should try to answer their questions. Parents should watch for signs that the child feels responsible for the person's death because of unkind thoughts or an argument preceding the death.

Preteens can learn about death when pets die. A dog's or cat's demise can provide parents with the opportunity to discuss death, to practice grieving, and to take part in funeral rituals. The same age-group also needs assurance that parents are feeling the loss, too, whether the death is of a pet or a human.

Teenagers sometimes cope by behaving in a way that parents find disconcerting, such as telling sick jokes. But those are signs of their anxiety. As with the other age-groups, discussion is essential. Allow the teens to express their feelings, share your own, don't judge how they should react, watch for signs that show they are having difficulty coping, and allow the grieving process time.

• **Adults and death**: I received a moving letter from an acquaintance, describing his father's death.

"We went down to Kentucky again, putting on a good send-off for my father," Harold writes. "After 79 years (some twenty of them with emphysema), he passed quickly and peacefully from our midst. It was a colorful life and decisively influenced more individuals than even he realized. My parents had a seventh-grade education but have always been known as being rather aware and articulate.

103

James Breig

"The funeral was conducted, suitably to his breadth of thought, by two Roman Catholics, a Lutheran and a Baptist. (The latter is) Mother's pastor, a friend of my parents who injected a reverently lighthearted note in a eulogy and led some prayers."

Harold's nephew and brother-in-law also spoke at "the almost tearless funeral. . . . The passing was just close enough to Christmas to enhance our Advent faith, yet just far enough from Christmas to let our friends and loved ones get over the initial loss. . . .

"The day after the funeral, I sat at his desk and at his typewriter that, after many years, had become mine. The graciousness of the folks in that little Southern town had made it a good place to live and, yes, a good place to die."

• **Taking over the funeral**: a friend told me the story of how some of his wife's relatives decided to make Uncle Luke's send-off something more than a run-of-the-mill ceremony.

"My wife's Uncle Luke died in his 90s," Dick tells me. "He ran a hardware store in a small town with one funeral parlor. He was the patriarch of a large family with a lot of children. When he retired, he became interested in gardening. His son, now in his 50s, had the responsibility of making the funeral arrangements. He went to the mortuary and said, 'We want to redecorate the place for the wake.' So all the relatives took everything out, recarpeted the place, brought in lawn furniture and a fountain, and made a garden out of the room where Uncle Luke would be laid out.

"Something about that caught the essence of the man, and it had an effect on the grieving people. Maybe we ought to look

104

Finding God in Your House

into that more," my friend concludes. "Maybe people should be waked in church or in a familiar setting rather than in a room no one's ever seen before."

Struck by the cutest girl

Dotty Epple died. The information came via my wife's high-school alumnae bulletin, which contained the notice: "It is with deep sorrow that I write to let you know that Dotty Epple Sheppard died suddenly, leaving behind her husband and 9-month-old daughter."

Dotty was my first crush. She never knew it, of course, because first graders don't announce such things. But I carried the torch for her at St. Ann's School. She was the cutest girl in class, made even cuter by her trademark: a streak of white, which cut across her dark hair. "The girl with the bleached streak" is how the alumnae journal described her, so I guess she still had that idiosyncrasy when she died.

I had not seen Dotty since we graduated in 1960, but the news of her death still touched me in a funny, acute way. It was another sign of my retreating youth and the onset of middle age. Hearing about contemporaries who have passed away is something older people experience, and now I'm experiencing it.

Life can leave at very inopportune times, like when you have a 9-month-old to care for or senior citizenship to look forward to or college tuitions to pay or vacation coming up. As I age, I recognize more and more the fragility of life; and I wonder why teenagers don't buckle their seatbelts and why kids ride their bikes like that and how come young couples don't lock their doors at night.

105

James Breig

Dotty's death gave me a November chill and one more reminder that people just never know.

In him we live, in him we die

As I write this, my friend Jon lies in the hospital with cancer; the prognosis is that he will live only two more years.

A week before he was his usual vital, energetic, always laughing, ready-to-help-out self. In less than a week, he had surgery for cancer that produced complications, which he nearly died from. Now he faces chemotherapy, orders from the doctor to become a recluse while other medication works on his bloodstream, and a deadline on his life.

My wife, Mary, has been crying a lot about Jon's condition. "Tell me why," she demands, "God does that to someone who is so Christian, who has devoted his life to the church, and who everybody is praying for?"

So I tried to answer. God didn't do it to Jon. The rain falls on the just and the unjust. Some things cannot be explained. God's will be done.

But she remains mad at God. Just as Jon was mad at him when Jon phoned me from his hospital bed to ask why he should go through chemotherapy. "I think I'll go to Hawaii and just lie on the beach until it's over," he said.

Two days later when I visited him in the hospital, Jon was more cheerful. And, in typical Jon-style, he announced, "They have an experimental program here helping terminal patients cope with their problems and understand what lies ahead. I think I can get involved in that. They're understaffed. I'm not a counselor; but I could talk to patients from my personal experience and say, 'I've been through it.' At least I'd be doing something positive.''

So maybe Jon has answered Mary's question. Maybe not. I do know that I believe what a mutual friend, a priest, said about Jon: ''When I think of living saints, I think of Jon.''

We'll be praying for him and for God's will to be done. But I always add a secret wish that a miracle might be in store.

CHAPTER 8

Families in (e)motion

Grandma to the rescue

Don't ever get a grandma angry. They can be tenacious, committed whirlwinds. That's the lesson I learned when I spoke recently with a grandmother about her teenage grandson. He calls her "Mee-Maw." She picked him up at school one day, and he made a startling request.

"Mee-Maw, I think I need to see a psychiatrist," he said. "Could you help me get an appointment?"

That he would be so honest shows just how strong his relationship is with her; it also shows how bad his relationship with his parents was. His grandmother knew that the teen had not been getting along with his mom and dad (Mee-Maw's son). But she hadn't realized how serious the problem had become. In fact, the teen was considering suicide.

So she sprang into action. She contacted friends, got the name of a psychiatrist, made the appointment, and began driving her grandson to the sessions.

"I put his picture on my mantle," she told me. "That kept him in mind. I kept that kid in my head for a year."

She also admits to "playing little tricks" to make sure the

appointments were kept. One time, when her daughter-in-law phoned to tell her that the boy was too busy with housework to keep one of the sessions, she listened politely, said okay, and hung up.

"Then I got in the car, drove over to my son's house and rang the doorbell," she said. " 'He's coming with me.' That's the last time they tried that."

As his parents withdrew more and more from their son, Mee-Maw filled the vacuum with her love. "I prayed for him, I listened to him talk until 3 in the morning, I'd go get him at school and take him to the doctor and stay there until he finished," she said. "He started calling me 'Sarge' because I didn't coddle him or say, 'Poor you.' I let him know he had some work to do and that he could do it."

Like all good grannies, she also ladled love out like chicken soup, surrounding him with her warmth.

There is no Hollywood ending to this story. This is, after all, real life. But the depressed teen on the edge of a breakdown graduated from high school and went on to college. His relationship with his parents didn't become Cleaver-ish, but he no longer felt like a nothing because of it. And, through it all, he had Mee-Maw. He had Sarge. He still has her to listen, to encourage and to pray with.

"I don't know why I'm telling you all this," Mee-Maw said to me when she finished her account.

I know why: so her example of dedicated, devoted and untiring love for the third generation would inspire other grandparents and so young people would know when things get tough with Mom and Dad there might be hope in a package labeled "Mee-Maw."

James Breig

Doesn't anybody stay in one place anymore?

If you had asked me a few years ago whether I liked living 500 miles from my parents and in-laws, I would have nodded vigorously, grinned widely and winked broadly.

Lately, though, I've reversed that attitude. I'm now willing to declare without hesitation that it's bad for families to live hundreds of miles from their roots.

Seventeen years ago, my wife, Mary, and I packed up two toddlers and moved nearly 500 miles from Ohio and from our parents, sisters and friends. We entered a new city in a new state and became strangers in our new neighborhood and at work. That's why for the first Thanksgiving and Christmas we drove back "home" to be with our relatives for the holidays. But a wintry round-trip of 1000 miles soon convinced us that we had to make our new house our new home. Besides, I argued, there's nothing unusual about our situation. I have a brother in Florida and sisters in Pennsylvania and Missouri. It's not like I'm the first to fly from the nest. This is called sharing the blame. But at that time I didn't see any blame. It was then that I could have argued convincingly about the value of being away from relatives. The advantages seemed obvious:

• We could create our own traditions. Take Christmas as an example. Instead of following the wishes and customs of our parents, Mary and I invented our own yuletide habits by selecting the best from what we had grown up with and combining those with what we wanted to do and what the kids contributed. The same applied to Thanksgiving, Easter, the Fourth of July, Labor Day, and every other occasion for family get-togethers.

So what if none of our relatives were present? After all, those

110

Finding God in Your House

who lived back in Ohio could participate through the loads of film we shipped to them, capturing every cute moment of every parochial school pageant.

• We could more easily come to our own identity and shape our family's future. Free from meddling relatives, advice-giving aunts, doting grandparents and nosy neighbors who "knew us when," we were able to shape our marriage and raise our children in our image and likeness.

• We could stay aloof from minor family quarrels and blowups. Obviously, major events like my parents' 50th wedding anniversary or my father's death drew us back to our roots. But we felt blessed not to be involved in the everyday problems that all families face. We could leave that to our siblings who had remained at the old homestead. They had to take elderly parents to the doctor and dentist; they had to sort out hurt feelings; they had to parcel their time so Mom and Dad couldn't claim "you haven't visited in two weeks."

I remember using those arguments on my friends Don and Lisa who constantly grumbled about having to spend holidays at Mom's, to be on call as Pop's taxi service, and to tolerate the interference of their parents. Eventually Don and Lisa moved nearly 700 miles away. But they have never let go of the apron strings and continue to make the grueling drive back home several times a year.

In contrast, it has been two years since Mary and I packed the kids into the car and put 500 miles on the odometer to see the old folks at home. One reason: those two toddlers we left Ohio with 17 years ago are now young men with jobs who can't get away for vacations.

But there is a third child, born away from her grandparents, a 10-year-old who has had no contact at all with our past lives. I've been thinking about that, and those thoughts have led me to change my mind. I wish we had stayed "home" or moved back or, at least, visited more often. When I realize that we have spent nearly two decades away from our respective parents, I worry about lost contact, missing memories and love that must, of necessity, be less intense. Absence does not make the heart grow fonder; it makes it grow forgetful. My earlier arguments about the advantages of living far from home are easily refuted because they are, when you think about it, so lame:

• Families can be shaped despite an uncle's free (although unrequested) advice; that's also part of growing up and maturing. I'd also ask why we young adults think we hold the franchise on wisdom and successful parenting. Where'd we come from? We also should give our children someone to run to when we're unjust, cranky and too stubborn to admit we're wrong.

• As for ceding the little nagging problems to our siblings, we should realize that being involved with the little problems isn't a burden at all but an opportunity. What excuses us from doing for our parents after all the years they did for us? Who took us to the dentist? Who wiped our noses and bottoms? Who held our heads when we upchucked? Who listened as we rambled on about life's unfairness because we didn't have a date for the prom or felt unloved or needed reassurance? Shrugging off such duties and moral obligations verges on the sinful. Taking distant delight in our siblings being stuck with Mom and Dad is just plain wrong.

Finally, don't forget this basic fact: it's as important to watch your parents grow old as it is to watch your kids grow up. Every mom and dad ends up saying, "Where did the time go? It was

Finding God in Your House

just a minute ago that the kids were crawling.'' So we struggle to find ''quality time,'' to take an interest in their activities, to put off work to play with them. But every adult also winds up saying, ''I never told my parents I loved them. I missed out on the chance to be their friends.'' We won't have to say that if we're around for their final years and actively involved in their lives.

I wonder—and worry—about the future. So many marriages are failing; so many children are growing up in single-parent homes or as stepchildren; mixed families with assortments of parents and grandparents abound; and, to top it off, ''moving' on'' and ''gotta go'' are the bywords of our upwardly and outwardly mobile society. Even when families remain intact, more and more they separate from their origins. In other words nuclear families are exploding, and extended families are becoming estranged—and both trends are booming. It's not right.

With everyone living 1000 miles from the place they grew up, who's going to keep track of the past, and who's going to plant the roots?

A rough day at the office

Did you ever go to your father's office when you were in grade school? Not many went to their mother's office in those days, because most mothers' offices were located in front of the washing machine. I used to go to my dad's work. Why I did it more than once I cannot fathom. It always happened in the summer, of course, after school had ended. Somehow, I would get the great idea that it would be jolly fun to spend the day with my dad.

113

James Breig

Spending a day with dad was fascinating for about the first 15 minutes when you got to meet his co-workers, sit at his desk, snoop around the cubbyholes, and work the water cooler (what great bubbles!). Unfortunately, his workday did not end at 9:15.

That meant I had to busy myself until noon when we would go to lunch at an actual restaurant. Staying busy in an office is not easy. Offices, for some reason, do not come equipped with crayons, train sets and baseballs. So I had to sit at an out-of-the-way desk, scribble on a piece of paper with a pencil and watch the clock. (What? How could it be only 9:18?)

Idleness soon led me to my father's office where I would stand and watch him work. This was about as intriguing as watching my toenails lengthen.

It was now a quarter to ten. . . .

Eventually, lunchtime rolled around and I got to tag along with the staff as they went out to lunch. This made the morning torture worthwhile. How often in the year did I get to go to an honest-to-gosh restaurant, order what I wanted, and listen in on grown-up chatter about sports? It was so delightful that I didn't give a thought to the fact that, after lunch, I still faced four hours of boredom.

And, boy, were they boring. There was no turkey sandwich and Coke to lure me on. There was just this endless ticking of the clock, each tick bringing a vow that I would never do it again.

Come to think of it, going to work then was a lot like going to work now.

If I've sufficiently frightened you away from bringing your child to work, don't be scared. According to an article in *Parents* magazine by two psychologists, taking a child to work can be

114

Finding God in Your House

beneficial. It gives the child a new view of mom or dad, eases uncertainty about where parents disappear to each morning, shows why parents aren't always available, and even helps explain why mom or dad are sometimes so tired at night.

To make the visit successful, the psychologists offered these tips.

1. Bring the child on an easy day, not when you are going to be swamped with work.

2. Let the child sit at your desk and pretend to be you. Assign him or her little chores like sharpening pencils, delivering messages, or running the copier.

3. Introduce your colleagues so the child can put faces to such terms as "the boss" or "my secretary."

4. Plan ahead and talk about what will happen.

5. If you don't work in an office, consider bringing your child for a tour of your workplace during off-hours or a holiday.

To all that I would add one very important point: Take a long lunch.

Please check your guilt at the door

Fortune magazine reports that "the number one cause of managerial guilt in America is the manager's perception that he's neglecting his family."

Now reread that quotation and include "she's" and "her" along with the masculine pronouns.

More and more families consist of two working spouses or single parents. In fact, in the last 25 years, those two categories have risen 221 percent and 430 percent respectively; while two-parent, one-paycheck homes have dropped nearly 60 percent.

James Breig

This has happened for a number of reasons. Divorced fathers have gained custody of their children; families need two paychecks to survive (or, at least, to "keep up with the Joneses"); women want to combine a career and homemaking, and more and more single mothers are the sole support for their children.

The inevitable result is pressure on the family, latchkey children, guilt for adults, distracted workers, strain on marriages, and government control of the home (through such things as day care).

There are grand solutions. Pope John Paul II has suggested that economic systems be overhauled so that families would not need two paychecks to get by. And the American bishops, in their economics pastoral, have asked for sweeping changes in society. But there are more immediate solutions:

• Examine your lifestyle to see how much you really need to survive and to enjoy life as opposed to consuming wildly and acquiring material possessions which you don't need.

• Discuss how you can balance your children's legitimate material needs—education expenses, for example—with their emotional requirements, such as a parent in the home when they are finished with school.

• Come to grips with sexist notions about who should work and who should run the home. If two paychecks are necessary, split the housework as well.

• See what employment solutions are available, such as split shifts, job-sharing and on-the-job day care.

• If you are a single parent, watch yourself for exhaustion from working, which can rob your children of the time they need with you. They will be happier with more of you and less of the net-worth line of your 1040 form.

Finding God in Your House

• Take full advantage of the time you do have with your children. Don't waste it in useless pursuits such as endless hours with the television.

• Make use of aids which are available from society or your parish or wherever. There are some helps—counseling, small groups, social programs—which can be an assistance. Don't ignore what already exists to lessen your guilt.

• Let your children in on what you do for a living so they don't feel a division between home and work, which pits one against the other. Take them to the office, show them what you use in your work, explain how you spend your day, discuss issues and problems you face, introduce them to co-workers.

These steps should help cut down on workplace guilt.

Friendship is the next-best thing to being there

"A friend in need is a pest."

That one-liner from an old-time comedian is funny, but it really misinterprets the cliché about "friends in need." The saying, "A friend in need is a friend indeed," doesn't mean that the friend needs something; it means that a friend who sticks by you when *you* are in need is a true friend. In other words, "a friend in your time of need is your friend indeed."

That came home to me recently during a period of personal distress when I was depressed and worried about the future. My concerns began to manifest themselves in lousy behavior at work and at home, where I became alternately a bear, a snake, a weasel, and a bull.

What returned me to human form were conversations with friends about my problems. They listened, advised, sympathized and generally soothed me. Without exception, they avoided riling me up, choosing instead to comfort me. When I would explain my predicament, they didn't try to do anything but give me room to let off steam and then offer some solutions to my dilemma.

In the past, friends would have done that in a living room or at the neighborhood tavern. But these are different days and my friends performed their sacraments of healing over the phone. From the Midwest, deep South and border states, they electronically showed me how deep their friendship ran.

Americans live in a mobile time and my friends are scattered across the nation. But geographical distance does not mean emotional distance. They stuck by me and nursed me through the hard times until I could be lived with again, and the problem, if not solved, lessened.

I bring this up to salute and thank them, but also to suggest that you may have a friend or relative hundreds of miles away who can help you. Or perhaps they could use your friendship. Don't let distance keep you apart.

CHAPTER 9

Faith matters

You're a pretty good person

When I'm in a really depressed mood (which, my wife tells me, is getting to be a bad habit with me), I total up the ways in which I have failed to live my faith. Then in an attempt to save myself from self-damnation, I begin to think of ways in which I practice my beliefs without even realizing what I'm doing. I'll bet you live out your Christianity without thinking about it because it has become ingrained in you and a part of your everyday actions.

Maybe it's time we stopped to think about how good we are instead of spending a lot of time denigrating the positive things we do and stressing the mistakes we make and the sins we commit.

Think about it: if you're married and have been faithful, that's the virtue of fidelity.

If you help your children with their homework and bring them treats, that's selfless love.

If you work hard for your employer, that's the virtue of justice. That same virtue is practiced by bosses when they treat their workers fairly. If you struggle to fix what's wrong with society by taking an active part in your community, that's another form of justice.

119

We should practice humility, but we should also recognize the virtues we have. At the same time, let's think about more everyday actions we can take to live our faith in simple yet profound ways. For example, do we look behind the faces of the strangers we see every day? In our daily lives, we encounter strangers all the time. There's the salesperson behind the counter, the man in the next booth at lunch, the woman who phones us at work, the people who pass us on the street.

Some of those strangers are in need materially. They are homeless, poor, addicted, neglected. Others are in spiritual need. They may have enough money, but they don't have enough friendship, love or understanding.

Jesus asked us to see him behind the faces of strangers. Do we follow that command? If we passed God on the street today, what would we say to him? How would we greet him? How would we treat him?

In a very real way, we do see God when we see strangers because each of us is made in his image. So the next time you encounter a stranger, pause a moment and think of what he or she needs from you. Perhaps it's your time and attention. Maybe it's your patience and understanding. It could be your concern and commitment. Whatever it is, see the face behind the stranger's and take a little extra time with that person.

Saints who aren't perfect

A bunch of us were sitting around one day debating two people who are often proposed as American saints-to-be: Thomas Merton and Dorothy Day.

Finally, one man said, "Do you realize something? Both of

them had illegitimate children.''

They did? It's public knowledge that Dorothy Day did, and it has long been rumored (but never proven) that Merton fathered a child before entering the monastery.

They wouldn't be the first saints with illegitimate children. St. Augustine comes to mind as an example from the past. And Merton and Day are known and should be celebrated for many other facets of their lives, including their work for peace.

But in this age of abortion, easy sex and out-of-wedlock births, the two of them would make interesting choices for canonization. The church would be saying that sanctity is not the same as perfection, and that sexuality doesn't disqualify men and women from being saints.

All the discussion over abortion puts a terrible onus of guilt on women. They should know that forgiveness is possible and reform encouraged. The stories of AIDS and herpes make sexually active people into modern lepers. They should know that chastity is possible. The canonizations of Merton and Day would be one way of making those points in a very public way.

Mass complaints

On a recent Sunday morning—if you can call 11 a.m. ''morning''—I was shaking my son Jim out of bed in order to get him to Mass on time. At 15 he is large enough to require a great deal of shaking before the message gets through the sleep to his brain. Finally, he slid the covers off his head and announced that he didn't have to go to church anymore.

''I've made my Confirmation,'' he argued, ''so I don't have to go.''

"Where'd you get that idea?" I asked.

"It's in the Bible," he replied, with only a slight hint of a question mark at the end of the sentence.

"Show it to me and you can sleep in," I said. "Until then, get up and get going."

As he and his brother, who is 14, enter those "do we hafta?" years, I find that I want more and more to make sure that we go to church as a family. Many different demands pull on each member of the family these days, and individuals like to go at times which appeal to them (I'm a Saturday-afternoon man personally). But now I'm starting my campaign to rope us all together for family Masses because I think that closeness adds to the meaning of the liturgy for children. If they go alone, there is a sense of isolation even in the most community-minded parishes (not to mention the temptation to skip out entirely and spend the time elsewhere).

Some teens say they go to Mass because of pressure from their parents. That sounds good enough to me. Don't give up out there. To make them go is not a cruel and unusual punishment. Remember the Bill Cosby line from his TV show when his daughter rejoiced at the removal of her braces and blamed her parents for making her wear them?

"Making you wear braces was not a punishment," Cosby told her. "If we hadn't, we'd live in a much larger house, and you would have teeth coming out your ears."

Ditto on the Mass. To make children go is not a punishment. If parents didn't do it, they might have less hassle in their lives; but their children would be deprived of something central to their existence: communion with God and with other believers.

Why do Catholics go to church every week? What's the point?

122

Finding God in Your House

Can't I speak to God by myself? I don't get anything out of Mass, so why should I go? Those are the questions that lie behind your children's weekly "Do we hafta?" when you say it's time to get ready for church. The next time you hear their question, try this story on them, told by a permanent deacon at a recent retreat:

A man named Jacob stopped going to the synagogue every week because he imagined some injustice against him by others. Perhaps there was an injustice and he deserved an apology. Either way, he quit going.

One evening, the rabbi came to visit him. As they spoke, the rabbi rose from the table and went to the fireplace. With tongs, he carefully removed a coal from the fire and placed it, alone, on the hearth.

Then he returned to the table. Jacob continued the conversation but kept his eyes on the coal, which slowly lost its glow and turned cold. Finally, it collapsed into a heap of ashes.

"I understand," Jacob said to the rabbi. "I'll be back at the synagogue next week."

The moral? Why not discuss it with your children and see what they say.

Parents admit they don't confess

Want to turn a Catholic's face as red as a cardinal's cape? All you have to do is ask one simple question: "When was the last time you went to Confession?" If the Catholic's face doesn't turn red, you will hear the following answer: "Uh . . . er . . . well. . . ."

Want to make a Catholic parent's eyes glaze over? Just ask

the following: "What example do you give your child when it comes to the use of the sacrament of Reconciliation?"

It's no secret that Confession (or Penance or Reconciliation) has become a little-used sacrament among many Catholics and that many Catholics would prefer not to discuss it because—ironically—they feel guilty.

Take Barbara as an example. The mother of five children, who range from 31 to 9, admits that she goes to Confession "as little as possible. I still have the attitude of getting in and getting it over with as fast as possible." While she has watched her youngest prepare for the sacrament in a positive manner, Barbara cannot bring herself to try face-to-face Reconciliation because she is so hooked on how she was trained as a child.

"Priests are a lot different now," she admits, "and children go frequently because the fear is not there for them." But the terror of the black box remains for her age-group.

Steve, a Midwestern father of six, remembers suffering from teenage scrupulosity and hitting the box as many as three times a week. His wife, Rose, visited the confessional monthly in her youth. With only one image of the sacrament—naming sins—they have found that it no longer meets their needs; and, today, they are annual visitors to the reconciliation room.

"The biggest reason I don't go," Steve explains, "is that it doesn't seem to meet any spiritual need I have, perhaps because it was overused when I was a youth. I just back away from it." Rose echoes his view, saying, "There's no need for it. I don't want to go to just any old priest." Nor will she go simply to set an example for her children. "Until I see that it's very important in my life," she says, "I don't think I should

Finding God in Your House

go.'' One result of that attitude is that their children are left on their own to go or avoid the sacrament.

What is interesting to discover is how little the sacrament is used by Catholics who are otherwise exemplary in their spiritual lives. Take Mike, a New Yorker who is active in peace and justice work, attends church regularly, was in the seminary, and now has four boys between 10 and 4. He even makes an annual retreat—which is the only time in the year that he goes to Confession.

His 10-year-old, Paul, like most children, has a better feeling about Confession than older Catholics. "I'd like to go more often," he says, "because I get a good feeling out of it."

Diane Vella, a religious educator at St. Barnabas Parish in Bellmore, New York, says, "People are funny about it. They are open to hearing about the new way we do it. But, when I get to the part when I tell them that it's primarily the parents' attitude that's going to influence the child, they're uptight, because they generally don't go."

By "generally," she estimates that three-fourths of the parents with children in the First Confession class who do not receive the sacrament themselves. "I can count on one hand those who go when we give them the opportunity during First Reconciliation. Catholics in general, no matter what side of the fence they're on, are uncomfortable with the sacrament," she says. "I try to listen to people to see where the anger is and where the hurt is. I suspect it's because of a bad experience."

Thomas Groome, associate professor of theology and religious education at Boston College, says "one crucial strategy" is to teach adults about Reconciliation to erase their image of Confession. "The new rite is tremendously positive, and adults shouldn't be allowed to regress to a juridical view of it. Parents want their children to go because they see some value in the sacrament, but they can't find it themselves. So the key is adult catechesis that revises the value of the sacrament."

That value, he says, lies in Reconciliation's power to help those "who want to grow in their faith, who want a source of healing, renewing, recommitment and peace. The parents didn't perceive that in the sacrament when they were children. They saw it as a painful process. We need to demolish that image and replace it with a sacrament of self-reflection, self-analysis, spiritual guidance and conversion."

Groome also stresses the importance of Catholics finding their own confessors wherever they can—"in the neighboring parish, in a monastery, in a house of prayer. It's not necessarily the same person for everybody."

Heaven is like a '32 Ford

This is what I think.

Heaven is like: heaven is like having a '32 Ford. And I mean having it.

What I mean is, if you ask people what they want the most in the world, they will probably name a particular thing. A single thing. Something they have kept in their heart or some secret place inside them. When you can get someone to tell you what their most wanted thing is, you learn something about them. An old woman might say, "I've always wanted to see Paris before I die." A middle-aged man might say, "I wish I could have played pro ball." Asked what he or she desires the most, a teenager might talk about a movie contract or world peace

Finding God in Your House

or a chance to write a song for Springsteen.

My Springsteen song, trip to Paris and movie contract is a '32 Ford. For as long as I can remember, I have thought that the cars made in 1932 were the most beautiful objects created since God rested on the seventh day. Just as the best sculpture came during the Renaissance and the top movies of all time were made in 1939 and the greatest baseball team breathed in 1961, the best automobiles came off the assembly lines in 1932. I think that God says on occasion, "This year, I'm going to let them glimpse Eden again."

Almost any '32 car would do for me, but I especially like the Ford Phaeton, a sleek vehicle of graceful lines and exquisite beauty. I remember, as a small boy (maybe as a first grader), coming home from a trip with my parents to find a gift from Gabby Hayes, then the host of a kids' TV show. I had sent away to him for models of antique cars, and they had arrived in my absence. It is my first memory of seeing heaven in the line of a fender.

Ever since, I have attended vintage auto shows, gazed at photos of Phaetons in catalogs with longing, and dreamed of having enough money to own one myself. My kids know about my mania for what they call "old cars" (pronounced as if it were one word: "olcars"). When we're out driving and one goes by across the median strip, headed, as always, away from me, everyone sings out, "Olcar, Dad."

I will never own a Phaeton. But I will continue to dream of climbing behind the wheel of one and tooling down a country road.

Life, it seems to me, is wanting a '32 Ford Phaeton. Heaven is getting one.

James Breig

Life is thinking about, dreaming about, wanting, longing for, reaching for, and accepting that the object of desire is just beyond our fingertips. Life is being sent pictures of the Eiffel Tower; it's being given a celebrity's autograph; it's watching a ball game on TV. That's life. But heaven is taking a vacation in Paris, signing an MGM contract, hearing Springsteen sing your composition, and having a chance to hum a fast one past the ear of Ted Williams.

Life is wondering about God. Heaven is getting God.

"Just this close" to God

Dave Stieb, a pitcher for the Toronto Blue Jays, might not appear to have credentials as a theologian, but something he said indicates that he has insight into people's relationship with God.

Stieb made his comment while being interviewed after he had won a baseball game against the New York Yankees. For the fourth time in less than a year, he had come close to pitching a no-hitter; this time, he had almost racked up a perfect game. But, with only a few outs to go in each game, a hitter had spoiled his bid for sports immortality. He had come, as they say, "just this close" each time, only to be denied.

The TV interviewer recounted those near misses and asked, "Do you ever feel that God isn't smiling on you for some reason?"

Stieb pondered the question. He must have been thinking about his career in baseball, his fame, his big-money contracts, and the constant praise he gets as one of his sport's best hurlers. Then he answered the interviewer's question: "I consider this smiling."

128

Finding God in Your House

Stieb had been tempted to blame God or the fates or bad luck for his failure to attain the no-hitter. Instead he looked at the positive side, and considered how far he had come and credited God with the blessings he had.

I wonder how many of us could use a dose of Dave-ology. How often do we moan and groan about what we don't have while we fail to thank God for all that we do have? I know I've fallen into the trap of wondering how I'm going to pay the mortgage this month or my son's college tuition next fall. Then I remember that I have a roof over my head and children I love—and so much more. And, beyond material goods, God has given me health, abilities and faith.

I consider that God is smiling a lot on me. He deserves more thanks than I give him.

Why is my mouth so big?

George Bush is not known as a spiritual adviser, but something he said during a recent interview made me sit up and nod vigorously because his experience is so close to mine.

He was asked what he was least proud of in his life. His reply: "Something I said to a classmate when I was 18. It hurt him very deeply."

I nodded because if I were asked the same question I would name several things that seem equally mundane and tiny but which are, nevertheless, things that have left me feeling the lousiest.

Some people, I suppose, can name huge sins and major crimes as their least proud moments but most of us muddle through life on a less grandiose scale. When I have sinned the worst,

James Breig

I think, is when I have been the smallest: hurling a one-line insult that cut too deeply, thinking a small-minded thought about someone else, failing to do something tiny that would have made a big difference to someone else, ignoring one of my children when they needed a hug or a compliment or an ear.

I don't think I'm being overly scrupulous about this (becoming what my father used to label as "a scroop"). I don't feel unforgiven; I just feel bad and weak and all too human.

Theologians will say that a whole bunch of venial sins do not add up to a mortal one. But, sometimes, they seem to weigh as much.

CHAPTER 10

From Lent to Christmas with the family

Maybe I deserve a break today

Here's a sentence I'm tired of hearing and saying: "I deserve it." It seems to have surreptitiously invaded the language as a statement of modern philosophy, one that justifies all sorts of sometimes neutral but frequently destructive behavior.

Some examples:

• I've said to myself when munching a second piece of carrot cake, "I deserve this because I skipped breakfast."

• I've heard my wife, Mary, say as she ignores housework, "I deserve a day off because I put in an extra hour at the office."

• Smokers say, "I deserve a cigarette; I'm tense."

• People will justify the purchase of an expensive plaything with: "I deserve this because I worked hard for the money."

This philosophy also gets expanded into "America deserves this because we're industrious; let the Third World suffer."

The opposite is also declared when disaster or distress strike: "I don't deserve this" or "What did I do to deserve this?"

The sentences bother me because I've come to realize they are so egotistical (all those "I's") and derive from self-centeredness. They assume that the world revolves around us. They remind me of the people who say that a friend's misfortune or illness teaches them how tenuous life is; therefore, there was meaning to that other person's woe. But what if they became someone else's lesson in life's vagaries? I suspect that they wouldn't accept being somebody else's reminder. Instead, they would wonder, "Why is God treating me like this? I don't deserve it."

Why do some people get delicious goodies while others are starving? No one deserves either. But those of us who got most of the former and then justify consuming still more on the basis that we deserve them ought to pause before the carrot cake goes in, the cigarette gets lit, or the Jaguar gets bought.

Just a thought for Ash Wednesday and the beginning of Lent.

Ready for a new-fashioned Lent?

We don't usually associate Lent and Easter with gift lists, holiday buffets and fir trees—but maybe we should. After all, such things give Christmas its special appeal. Maybe if we could link them with Lent, our observance of these six weeks would take on extra meaning.

Of course, we'd have to sacrifice some things—Lent's emphasis on forgiveness, for instance; or its theme of reconciliation between God and us and between us and our fellow human beings or Lent's period of reflection and renewal.

But maybe we could combine all these elements and come up with a new way of looking at Lent. Maybe we could use those gift lists, buffets and trees after all—but in a very Lenten way:

Gift lists: draw up a list of your friends, relatives, family members, neighbors, and co-workers. What Lenten gifts could you give them? Could you pray for them more fervently after Communion? Could you offer forgiveness to someone who has

Finding God in Your House

been estranged from you? Could you seek forgiveness from someone you offended? Could you come up with plans that apply God's will to your community in service to the poor, handicapped, or neglected?

Buffet: go ahead and make plans to invite your friends or family to a big holiday banquet. But, instead of a table laden with goodies and treats, have everyone select from a spiritual smorgasbord: reflection on Jesus; prayer for world peace; meditation on our sins; discussion of how to apply Christian principles to the neighborhood, workplace or home. Or how about a sacrificial meal for your family with the money not spent on food donated to a local food pantry or organization that fights world hunger?

Easter tree: this season is connected with the most famous tree in history—the one on which Jesus hung for three hours. Is there a crucifix in your home? If there is, how often do you look at it? Where is it displayed? When do you meditate on Jesus' suffering? Could you imitate his sacrifice for others? If your home has no cross, why not?

Pick one of the above ideas for your Lenten exercise this year. If you follow through, you'll arrive at an Easter that is as joyous as any Christmas morning.

Lent: time to forgive and forget

What to do for Lent now that it's under way.

That's what I was thinking about, both for myself and for you. I don't want to get preachy with you. Most of you probably do far more for Lent than I do and could offer some great suggestions.

James Breig

Then I had an idea: What about ideas themselves? What if I just offered some ideas that would help you to think? What if I gave us all some spurs to meditation, prayer, and taking stock of who we are? After all Lent is a time for disassembling ourselves and seeing what parts work, which ones need oil, and where we could use some replacements.

So here are some ideas I've collected. You might want to select one or two and do some serious thinking and talking about them:

1. I've heard a lot of Catholics whine about their youth and how the nuns who taught them messed up their notions of sex, authority and God. I always wonder when they're going to let go of the past. At some point, they've got to stop fixing blame on "Sister" and examine their own responsibilities.

It's the same with our parents. I am as quick as anyone to lay blame at my parents' door for my phobias (dentists and hospitals, for instance) and compulsions (everything on my plate has to be in the same location every night: meat in the upper-right quadrant). But I'm much slower at complimenting them for the good things in my life for which they are responsible: my notion of the sanctity of marriage or my ideas on the dignity of all human beings.

This Lent might be a good time for all of us to let go of past blames, to take responsibility for what we are, and to change what we don't like about that. We could also take time to credit our parents, the nuns at school, and other influences on us for the positive traits and beliefs in our lives.

2. "As a culture, we're working pretty hard to keep our bodies in shape," notes Father Kenneth Alt, associate pastor of Immaculate Conception Parish in Celina, Ohio. "But are we also working to keep ourselves in good spiritual condition?"

134

Finding God in Your House

For its Lenten program, that parish has tried to link the two, according to the *Catholic Telegraph,* newspaper of the Cincinnati archdiocese.

What if we even out the time we spend on physical and spiritual health this Lent? How much of our day or week goes into dieting, athletes, walking for fitness, aerobics and so on? Do we spend an equivalent amount of time praying, reading spiritual material and reflecting on our relationship with God?

3. A recent TV special examined the values, hopes and goals of the '60s. At the end of the show, a film clip of the Beatles singing "All You Need Is Love" was played. As the music continued, participants in the program were asked if the song's message was still valid. Is love all we need? I found the responses very interesting and revealing.

Ex-Beatle George Harrison declared, "Yes, absolutely." But his former partner Paul McCartney said, "I don't know." An activist from the '60s replied, "No. It's nice, as is peace. But justice is all you need" (thus unconsciously echoing Pope Paul VI, who said, "If you want peace, work for justice").

A poet, asked if love is all we need, answered, "You need truth," while another person turned practical and said, "You need sobriety, a lot of positive energy, and to know where your next meal is coming from."

Still another observer said that it was easy for the Beatles to decide that love was all they need because "they are rich and talented."

How would you answer that question? Is love all we need? What is love?

4. Writing in *U.S. Catholic* magazine, Dolores Curran, an author and columnist who focuses on family life, listed "seven

135

James Breig

serious sins of somewhat saintly children.'' These are ''things about children that I do not like,'' she wrote, and the list provides parents and children with some discussion topics for Lenten suppers. Here they are, with some comments from Curran:

- **Disrespect** ''for others, for their own selves, for property, and for things religious seems to be part of childhood today,'' she writes. ''It shows up in nasty retorts, fighting between siblings, behavior toward adults, disregard for property, and drug and alcohol abuse.''

- **Hedonism**: Healthy families ''teach that happiness does not lie in the accumulation of goods and gratification but in relationships and work satisfaction.''

- Irresponsibility: ''Some parents feed into children's irresponsibility when they nag and take on Scout projects, homework, and other responsibilities that belong to children.''

- **Sloth**: ''One of the duties of parents is to rear fit children. If parents turn their children over to television and refuse to give them opportunities to prove their abilities, parents neglect an important area of child development.''

- **Distrust**: Parents deal with this by inflicting ''a consequence on early lies and deceptions but give their children a second chance. Just as in our relationship with God, broken trust is not forever.''

- **Jealousy**: ''Effective parents tend to encourage the effort rather than the achievement. . . . These parents also prize uniqueness over conformity in children, which minimizes jealousy.''

- **Negativism:** ''This includes skepticism, cynicism, lassitude, and hopelessness. . . . Healthy families foster an attitude of optimism and hope that spills over to their children.''

Curran notes that one way for children to get rid of these faults is for parents to be role models of the opposing virtues. How are you doing with that assignment?

In the old days, we used to give up some type of food for Lent. Perhaps some of the above will give you food for thought. If so, eat all you want.

Thank God, it's Good Friday

If it weren't for Easter, we wouldn't call Good Friday good. If Jesus had died and disappeared on Friday, it would be a day of mourning only—not a day to be considered positive.

When the nation marks the anniversary of the Friday on which John F. Kennedy died, no one suggests labeling that date ''Good November 22.'' In fact, many people object to our marking that date at all. If you want to honor the man, they argue, do so on his birthday, as we do with Lincoln, Washington and King.

We mark such birthdays because they are positive events, dates when great people came to us and began their lifework. Can you name the date on which Abraham Lincoln died? In contrast, everyone knows he was born on February 12.

Why is Jesus different? We celebrate his birthday, of course, but the church always emphasizes that Easter is a greater feast than Christmas. And Easter makes the Friday he died ''good.'' How come?

The answer is not difficult to understand. We all have our ''Christmases'' and ''Fridays''; that is, we are all born and we all die. But until Jesus and Easter, human beings thought that was all we had—birth and death. We didn't know about heaven,

God's goodness to us, the afterlife, the promise of eternal joy with the Creator, the triumph of goodness over evil, the victory of life over death.

Christmas is great and Friday is good because the second person of the Trinity did two wonderful things: he emptied himself to become human at his nativity, and he died for our sins on Friday.

No wonder Easter is triumphantly and spectacularly joyous. Jesus did one more wonderful thing: he came back to tell us about everlasting life.

Because of that, we can face all that lies between our birth and our death: all the suffering and pain, all the disappointment and failure, all the heartache and grief. We know now that it will all be made right in the next world if we follow the example of how Jesus lived between his Christmas and his Friday.

But I meant . . .

Carrie, our 10-year-old, and I began discussing Jesus being both human and God. I was quizzing her on what she understood about that mystery, and it turned out to be a lesson on Easter and a lesson in humility for me.

Me: Is Jesus a man or God?

Carrie: He's a . . . wait a second. Are you going to write about this?

Me: No. (And, for the moment, I meant it. But I didn't know what lay ahead.)

Carrie (looking doubtful): Well, okay. He's God.

Me: Half right. He's both a man and God. Is he alive or dead?

138

Finding God in Your House

Carrie: Alive!

Me: Right. Very good. That's what we celebrate at Easter. Some people think we should celebrate Easter with more excitement than Christmas because everyone was born, but only Jesus rose from the dead. But he couldn't have done that if he hadn't been born; so Christmas is important, too. And his birth is really important because it was the only time God was born as a human. . . .

My lecture continued for a few more minutes, and then it was time to wrap it all up for her. So, putting on my best daddy-professor tone, I decided to end our conversation by making a point about how Jesus acted when he was on earth. Of course, I chose the wrong phrase and got caught.

Me: So, Jesus, both a man and God, when he was alive. . . .

Carrie (interrupting): But he's still alive!

Me (fumbling): Yes, well, I meant when he was on earth. . . .

Carrie (delighted): But he's here now, too, in Communion. And you said "alive." You were wrong. He's still alive. I got you! I got you!

Me (looking around to make sure there were no witnesses): But I meant. . . .

Carrie (triumphantly): I gotcha!

Me: Okay, Carrie, you got me. But now I've got an article. . . .

Banana bread

Here's a post-Easter thought: the perfect symbol of the resurrection is banana bread.

Don't believe it? Think it over: bananas rot and die, seemingly useless except as garbage. But they can be reborn into a great dessert when they are used to make banana bread.

The next time someone suggests the caterpillar and butterfly as a resurrection symbol, try banana bread on them.

First things later

On the night before her First Communion, I asked Carrie to write down how she felt. She wrote:

"How I feel: Scared, happy, excited, proud."

She defined First Communion pretty succinctly, as "a time when boys and girls get ready for their First Communion."

I can't add much to that, Carrie. I will say how proud I was of everyone involved in your First Communion. The emphasis was properly placed on the importance of the occasion, and no one tried to pretend it was anything but a significant moment in your spiritual life. That included everyone from your religious education teacher to the people who came to the party and brought gifts with religious meaning to them: Bibles, rosaries, a plaque reminding you how important everyone is as God's children, a cross on a chain for you to wear as a sign of your beliefs.

Most of all, of course, I was proud of you. You managed to overcome your fears of the day and to look beautiful, sing your hymns loudly, carry up your gift proudly, and receive Jesus humbly. Everyone who was there felt so close to you and loving; I hope you felt that, too.

It's good to be in church with you now and to know you will walk to Communion with us, instead of staying behind. Jesus, you know, asked for the little children to come to him; and they

140

shouldn't be left in the pews while grown-ups receive him on Sunday.

So, welcome again to the church (you don't remember the first welcome—at your Baptism). Your family is proud of you.

M is for the many things she gave me . . .

When mother celebrated her 80th birthday, I asked her what sort of parties she had as a child, and she told me that she didn't remember ever having a birthday party as a little girl. She did recall outhouses, however, sooty train rides, and a man who came courting her sisters. His pockets were laden with what they called Hershey buds ("kisses").

The man would reach in his pocket and toss a handful of the buds on the table, a sign of how sweet he was on one of the sisters, although my mother is not clear on which one he fancied. She does remember the buds quite vividly, however. She also remembers how the man, when the time came for his departure, would snatch up the remaining candies and return them to his pocket.

This same man, one Christmas, arrived with three huge, round, bright red apples, which he placed on the table. The entire family oohed and aahed over the shiny fruit, a rare and succulent treat. But, as before, when it came time for the man to leave, he picked up two of the apples, returned them to his lonely pockets and, tipping his hat, left.

That man never became my uncle, a tribute to the wisdom of my mother's sisters.

A lot of my mother's memories were like that: simple, humble, unpretentious, and, very often, revelatory of human be-

James Breig

havior; she had the ability to assess a person in about 30 seconds. When she pronounced someone a horse's behind (one of her favorite labels), he or she invariably whinnied.

I don't have that knack; I am constantly reevaluating what I think of people. (I'm still not entirely sure, for instance, that Attila was such a bad guy.) But I have inherited my mom's simplicity. A Hershey bud is more precious to me than caviar and champagne. A baloney sandwich is heaven.

This Mother's Day, think about what your mother gave you, which virtues of hers you wish you had, and how long ago it was that you last told her you loved her. Narrow that time gap.

And when you see her, leave all the apples behind.

Slow down; you move too fast

I was chatting with Sue recently. She and I work in the same building, and she had two children graduating from high school. Beaming, she showed me their yearbook photos and talked about their achievements. Then her glow diminished a little as she talked about the double expenses of two graduations. "At least I can save money by having one party," she said. I noted the advantage of getting both events over with at once. My sons graduated in back-to-back years. Then we talked about what gifts parents consider appropriate for graduations.

"I can't believe," Sue said, "how many people give their kids cars. Forget it! We used to get watches and bikes for high-school graduation. Now they give those to kindergarten grads."

We laughed; Sue threw a dismissive hand at overspending parents and she was off to show her photos to someone else. When she was gone, I began thinking about how often I have

Finding God in Your House

tried to rush my children into experiences they weren't ready for. I wasn't thinking about material things, such as Porsches for 17-year-olds or Rolexes for kindergarteners. I was thinking about times I have tried—for the best of motives—to introduce my children to good experiences they just weren't old enough for.

An example: when I was in high school, I saw "To Kill A Mockingbird." It was a movie that contributed greatly to my character and my beliefs. Films like that one, "The Miracle Worker," and "Judgment at Nuremberg" didn't shape who I am, but they did affirm and support and ratify. So, a few years ago when those movies came on television, I tried to get my sons to watch them. But they were only in grade school at the time. In addition, the era had changed. The message of "Mockingbird" means one thing in the middle of the civil-rights movement; it means something else two decades later. But I wanted them to experience what I experienced. They didn't, and I felt bad.

I think parents do a lot of that: rushing children into feelings that we had but that we cannot possible duplicate for them. They'll have their movies and moments and movements; they'll have their affirmation and support and ratification; they'll experience exhilaration and joy and inspiration. If we're lucky, we'll be there to see it or we'll see it on their faces afterward. Maybe we can point them toward the right experiences, but we can't force them.

It's the same with religion. How many parents disappoint themselves by trying to photocopy their understanding of Jesus and prayer and faith onto their children? Maybe First Communion or Confirmation or Christmas Midnight Mass were high

143

points for us; that doesn't mean our children will feel the same spiritual thrill when they attend those liturgies. But they might find God in their First Penance or at a charismatic prayer service or during a friend's wedding.

I bet there's not a parent anywhere who hasn't taken his or her child somewhere and said, "Isn't this great?" only to have the child answer with a shrug. It's not a rejection; it's a declaration of independent feeling. Parents shouldn't feel rejected when it happens; they should feel delighted that they have created an individual distinct from themselves.

Fathers don't always know best

I recently talked with several dads about the changing role of fathers in American society. They listed a lot of positive changes, such as husbands who share child rearing equally with their wives and men trying to overcome the weaknesses they saw in their own dads. But when I asked them what they rely on as guidance for their parenting, the fathers were at a loss to name anything besides instinct.

All sorts of printed resources exist to help fathers, but the dads I talked to recommend something that can't be found on bookstore shelves. "I use a lot of trial and error," Dave admits. He pooh-poohs books on parenting because "most assume that the father isn't interested in being a father and has to be controlled into doing it. Mostly, I rely on images of God in the Bible and the ambiguous figure of Saint Joseph. It's great that you can fill in the blanks on him. He had a sense of letting God guide him when he was put into a difficult situation."

Finding God in Your House

Chris also recommends a good dose of intuition as guidance. "I raised animals as a child," he recalls. "When my first son was born, I told my mother, 'I'm afraid I'm not going to love my child as much as I loved those animals.' But I simply am myself. I'm comfortable holding them and caring for them." Steve didn't do much reading either; rather, like Chris, "I relied on what came naturally from my own experience growing up. But my primary source is probably the Bible and looking at the relationship Jesus has with his children—us."

Greg makes it up "as I go along. I wanted to be a father who was involved. The only time my father fed a child a bottle was when he gave one to my son." Larry scorns books on parenting because "I'm not convinced anyone can write a book to make someone something he's not already. I go by the good examples of fathers I know. I also went to my past and judged what I missed as a kid and work hard to overcome those shortcomings."

I asked the fathers if they talked to their own dads, older brothers or peers about being a parent; they said no. They have ignored other resources around them—books, magazines, the experience of others—in favor of just making it up as they go along.

I'm lucky. I never conversed with my father about being a dad, but he wrote books on being a parent. I read those throughout my youth, adolescence and early adulthood; so I knew his philosophies of raising children. Through the years, I have also written numerous articles about being a father, which means I have interviewed experts in the field. I'm not praising myself here; if it weren't for my father's writing and my own, I'd be relying on guesswork as much as the other dads.

145

James Breig

Why is that? Why do moms subscribe to magazines about being mothers and read books on child development and get together with other women to discuss their kids while the pops are arguing about who was better, Mickey or Willie? It isn't that the men don't care; my interviews with fathers found guys who care a great deal about their relationship with their children. I think dads don't go beyond instinct for the following reasons:

1. Their fathers never subscribed to a newsletter for dads. The old man read the *Sporting News* and *Outdoor Life*. If that was good enough for him, it's good enough for me.

2. Reading books, magazines, newsletters and articles about something as sensitive as children is not macho. Flying by the seat of your pants is manly. Men never ask for directions when they're driving; why would they when they're raising kids?

3. Talking to other men about parenting betrays a weakness on your part and assumes someone else can tell you something you don't know. Both of those are tough for guys to do.

4. Looking for help in being a dad proves that you are a sensitive, loving person who cares about his children and their future. Many men don't want to be caught with their defenses down.

This Father's Day, I have a suggestion for readers. If you're a wife, make sure your husband reads this article. Then talk to him about how he has learned to be a dad and how he plans to improve himself. If you're a dad, think about what resources you rely on to be a good father; maybe you could be a better one by talking to someone else or reading more. If you're a grandpa and have some wisdom to impart, talk to your son about being a father, but don't be pushy.

Finding God in Your House

My sparkling life as a firework

Our daughter, Carrie, 10, has shown leanings toward writing, and one of her recent endeavors takes an unusual look at the Fourth of July. She titled it "Boom! Bang!" I told her that if a college graduate showed me this work, I'd hire him or her as a reporter. See what you think:

"It was the 4th of July. I was being loaded into some boxes. Excuse me, I forgot to introduce myself. I'm a firework. My name is Sparkle. You see, I am one of those fireworks who sparkle down like fairies.

"Well, anyway, this is the last two hours of my life. Once I'm fired off, I die. Oh, please, no sympathy. Yes, I know, it is sad. But that's how the bang goes.

"About two hours later, I was being aimed at the stars. Then they set fire to me and I was up in the sky. What a gorgeous sight. All of a sudden, I turned into sparkles. I died in the sound of oohs and ahhs.''

One less son to pick up after

Every year since 1974 my wife, Mary, and I have risen early on a certain September morning. It's usually nippy outside with a thick dew on the grass, but we venture outdoors for a ritual that has many years to run.

The September day is the first day of school, and the ritual is the filming of our children going off to class.

We began the ceremony when our oldest son, Jimmy, went to kindergarten. He went with a smile on his face and a Mickey

Mouse bookbag in his hand—after we had fished him out from beneath his bed. He waved gaily as he boarded the bus. We found out later that the bravado faded at school, where he spent hours crying in the principal's office.

This month that little boy is a college freshman, and his mother will probably be the one crying. (At a Mass marking his high-school graduation, the students at his school brought their mothers a rose. When Jimmy arrived at our pew with his flower, Mary burst into tears. The woman in front of us turned around and asked, "Your first?" When Mary nodded, the woman noted her own dry eyes and said, "My last.")

The filming continued through the years as Matthew, a year younger than Jimmy, joined his brother on those September mornings, each boy holding up fingers to indicate which grade he was off to. Eight years later, their sister joined them in the rite of fall.

The old movie camera, the same one that filmed Mary's high-school graduation, rattles and ticks as it does its work. And getting the film developed takes forever because no one works with that format anymore. But we press on with our tradition, ignoring the video craze and putting onto celluloid the images of growing children, images which become more valuable with each passing September.

More than just a trick or treat

A friend of mine thinks that autumn is the best season. I don't know that I have a favorite among the four seasons. Each has its own special pluses, although the best I can say for February is that it is mosquito-less. But it's not a season anyway.

I like the fall for its clichés—crisp air, apple cider, colorful

Finding God in Your House

leaves (when I don't have to rake them), the World Series (especially in seasons without strikes), kids going back to school with brand-new lunch boxes, the surprise visit of Indian summer.

Fall also has Halloween. I like Halloween. My wife is great at coming up with wacky costumes for the kids. If it were left up to me, I would do one of two things, both of them blasphemous. I would either go out and buy plastic costumes that turn my children into cartoon characters, or I would rely on the old standbys—burnt cork for beards and old clothes that result in the hobo look.

Mary won't settle for that. She's come up with some great costumes over the years. The best was the time she suited Matthew (then about 10) in baseball regalia and colored his face red. She hung a sign around his neck, "Embarrassed Yankee." That Halloween was just after the Yanks had lost to the Dodgers after winning the first two games and then dropping four in a row. People couldn't get enough of that costume; Matt was invited into homes to show others his mother's ingenuity, and everyone had a good laugh.

Halloween has gotten a bad name in recent years among those Catholics influenced by fundamentalism. They see the holiday as somehow celebrating witches, the devil and death. In fact, it does precisely the opposite. By making fun of death, Halloween celebrates the eternal life that Christ made possible. Halloween laughs at death and says, "You lose."

I like the autumn. Where's my rake?

Thanksgiving: no turkey of a feast

Americans have some great holidays. I don't know about Bastille Day in France and Guy Fawkes Day in England, but I do know that I'd be happy to match them up against the Fourth of July and Thanksgiving. They have become family-reunion days when the materialism that can infect Christmas is missing and the mixed emotions about Easter are absent.

Thanksgiving, which also has no militaristic taint, is especially welcome. It's a day for getting together with friends and relatives, to reflect on the best things in life and to realize that they are not possessions, to include God in the most mundane events (like eating and watching football on TV), and to simplify.

Thanksgiving has escaped those scars that sometimes mar other holidays. Christmas has its rush, New Year's has become a day for drunks and hangovers, Valentine's Day is now pretty phony, and Easter needs to be reworked. But Thanksgiving has retained its pristine purpose. No one goes decorations-crazy; most people don't use it as an excuse to get loaded; it's short and thus evades the problems of holidays that stretch on and on . . . and on.

Thanksgiving is pure. It's placed nicely in the year, before horrible weather and after the summer doldrums; it provides everyone with an okay to be thankful to God in public, and it brings together families without danger of rancor over forgotten gifts or visits that last too long.

I like Thanksgiving for all those reasons. I guess I could say that I am *thankful* for Thanksgiving.

Prayer from the mouths of babes

Our 8-year-old, Carrie, wrote this Thanksgiving prayer for use just before the turkey is served:

"I am sorry for my sins. I forgive Jimmy and Matt (her older brothers) when they hurt me. And love as I should. Amen.

Finding God in Your House

"Thank you for mom, dad, Matt, Jimmy. They been so kind to me. Mommy and daddy are the best parents in the world. I hope every boddy in the world have a happy thanksgiving. The End."

That prayer brims with wisdom. She forgives others while also admitting her own sinfulness. She promises to do better and expresses appreciation for all the really good things in her life (no mention, for instance, of toys and clothes and TV). Then she extends her prayer to encompass all of humankind. It seems to me that the last prayer to contain all those elements was the "Our Father."

This Thanksgiving, why not ask one of the littler ones in your life to compose the dinner-table prayer? You could do a lot worse with some of the "official" compilations of jargon and two-bit words which sometimes pass for heartfelt prayers.

It's beginning to look a little like Christmas

I don't know a single Catholic in the world who would say, "I overprepare spiritually for Christmas during Advent."

They do say it when they refer to buying gifts, sending out cards, or decorating the house. But spiritual preparation usually is lost in the holiday rush. Catholics regret missing out on Advent. To avoid that mistake again this year, plan right now to make this Advent a good one. Then, in January, families will be able to look back at December and say, "We made it."

Here are some ideas on how to make Advent work without neglecting all the usual Yule duties:

1. Pick one day of the week during Advent to do something extra spiritually. Go on; name the day and mark it on the calendar. Maybe you will go to Mass on Wednesdays or say morn-

151

ing prayers on Mondays or switch off the tube on Fridays in order to read the Bible or some other spiritual work.

Whatever it is, pick the day and the activity now. Do it before going on to #2.

2. Go back to #1 and *do* it. Now mark it on your December calendar. I'll wait.

3. Now here's another idea: make the usual Christmas preparations into spiritual occasions. For example, instead of routinely addressing cards, why not say a prayer for each person as well? You have a list of people you care for; so go ahead and recite a prayer for them as you lick the envelope. Maybe it could be something simple, like, "Lord, bless this person and keep her in your grace in the coming year." Make up a prayer. It will add to the Advent season.

4. Make use of one of the religious traditions of the season, such as the Advent wreath. Or how about the one that involves the creche? In that one, add a piece of straw to the creche for every good turn done during Advent. That way, Christians literally and figuratively prepare for Jesus' arrival. In place of real straw, use strips of newspaper or even Easter-basket stuffing (that would make a nice connection between the two Christian feasts, which depend on each other and which mark the two major events in Christ's life).

5. Slow down. I recently saw the results of a survey of Catholics regarding Christmas, and again and again, they said they would like to relax more during the holidays so they would have more time to prepare spiritually for Christ's nativity. So why not add to Advent by subtracting from Christmas? Stop doing something that doesn't *have* to be done. Bake two dozen fewer cookies . . . string one fewer row of lights . . . skip the out-

door finery . . . eliminate some cards. That way, families will have more time to sit back and reflect on the meaning of Christmas.

6. Select something positive to do for someone less fortunate during the four weeks of Advent. Maybe it could be something every day or something once a week until Christmas. Homes for the elderly would like volunteers; the lonely person down the block could use one of those fruitcakes—and a friendly presence for a chat; somebody in the hospital would like to hear from you by telephone. If you do just one thing during December that you have not done before, you will be happier and someone will be better off. That's a pretty good bargain.

7. If you're a grandparent, send your children film for their cameras right now and tell them to mail the exposed film back to you for developing. Voila! You have photos of the grandkids, you have made life easier for your children at this time of year, and you have connected with your family in a unique way.

8. Arrange an operator-assisted conference call among members of your family who haven't chatted in a while.

9. Check your diocesan newspaper for a Christmas or Advent event and take the family to it. You'll combine an outing, a break from the Christmas rush, family togetherness, getting to know new people and a spiritual exercise. Not bad for one night, right?

10. Invent one new family tradition for the holidays. Take nominations from all members of the household.

11. Gather the clan together and have everyone tell a story of a past Christmas. It could be a silly moment, a sad time, a warm memory or a great gift. Whatever, relive those moments as a family.

12. Do something childish. Go sledding, skiing, hayriding; play Monopoly or hopscotch; attend the Disney movie in town; form your own caroling group.

13. Have everyone write down when they felt closest to Jesus during the past year or so. Save the papers and read them at Christmas dinner or before opening presents.

Let's keep the innkeeper

He's usually put on a par with Judas and Pilate or at least Peter for weak-kneed characters in the Gospels, but the innkeeper who gave Mary and Joseph a Christmas Eve cave should be a holiday model for Christians celebrating the birth of the Messiah. That's because that Middle East Howard Johnson had the simple consideration to think beyond the "no" which could have easily been his complete conversation with the visiting strangers who came to his door.

Put yourself in the situation of the innkeeper. It's a chilly night, the town is loaded with strangers for the census, your rooms are full of carousing soldiers and tax collectors, you've run out of food for the third sitting of supper, and the wine barrels are nearly drained. There's a rap on the door. Now what? It's a poor couple with a donkey. He's haggard and she's—yipes—she's pregnant. They want a room. Big surprise! So does the rest of Israel.

Consider your options: shut the door in their faces, say "no way, Jose and Maria," or take a moment to think. Yeah, there is that space in the cave where the animals are.

So you linger at the door, give them directions, and feel good about yourself.

Finding God in Your House

Does that sound like betraying Peter, traitorous Judas or lily-livered Pilate? Or does it sound like everyday Christians? Does it sound like something they could do this Christmas? Maybe someone extra could be included at their holiday table. Not just friends and co-workers and neighbors and relatives, but people on the outs, people no one thinks of the rest of the year, people who need a little touch of the innkeeper's hospitality.

What people? People like the widow down the street, the senior citizens in the home nearby, the homeless family living in the shelter downtown, the poor child with no toys, the forgotten neighbor, the handicapped veteran in the hospital. They could all use some holiday warmth and cheer and closeness.

Many institutions offer programs to introduce better-off Christians to the modern-day equivalents of the pregnant lady and her husband from 2000 years ago. Churches can link parishioners with needy families, not just to give them gifts but to invite them into a home. Cities often sponsor programs to bring food to the hungry; why not bring the hungry to the food? Big Brothers and Big Sisters, welfare agencies, programs sponsored by religious groups, drives run by newspapers—those are all sources of getting Christians to the people who need their Christmas spirit this year.

If Christians do it, it could be the best Christmas of their lives and give new meaning to the celebration of Jesus' birth. It could remind Christians why they are his followers and teach their children about charity. It could give an example to others for them to try, renew a guest's sense of dignity, give action to Christian words about selflessness, and inspire others to practice more works of mercy.

If all Christians did something extra for just one person this

Christmas, wouldn't the holiday be much nicer, more memorable and closer to what Jesus came among us for? And imagine how much Jesus would like it if everyone took in a stranger, just like the innkeeper his parents surely used to tell him about when he was a toddler.

Lights, ornaments, blessing

When you finally get the tree into your house and standing up straight and in no danger of toppling onto the couch, why not bless it as a family with this little poem? Here's what to do: gather everyone around the tree, either before or after decorating it, and recite this benediction. You could have one person say the blessing or it could be done as a group. You could also have different people take a line or stanza. Use your imagination. Here's a blessing for the Christmas tree:

Bless this tree and all those near it;
Bless our blessing when you hear it;
Bless the stump and bless each limb out;
Bless us as we sing a hymn out;
Guard this tree and us who love it;
Guard the ceiling just above it;
Guard the floor and, we desire,
Guard the house from any fire.
Bless each bulb and every candle;
Bless each ornament we handle;
Bless us as we light and trim it;
Bless us, Lord, without a limit.

Finding God in Your House

All wrapped up in the present

Some quick images of Christmases past and present come to mind:

• My wife, Mary, painstakingly wrapping gifts. She sits on the floor surrounded by tape, ribbons, paper, boxes, tags, and presents. I can wrap a gift in two minutes, and it looks it. But Mary puts her love for people into the visible forms of colored paper and bright bows. It's something I admire.

• How seldom we buy Christmas gifts that have anything to do with Christ. The slogan is "put Christ back into Christmas." How about putting him into what we buy? What percent of the presents given every year have anything to do with the season? Religious books, cards, posters, and statues are rarely among our pile of presents. How about yours?

• Guilt buying. Last year, Mary and I went to a little gift shop to buy knickknack gifts for neighbors, co-workers, Carrie's teacher, and so on. Even the cashier couldn't believe the final total: $200. She double-checked everything to make sure. That amount is a sign of how easily we fall prey to "add-on" gifts: those little items that we think, collectively, show our feelings for other people. Thus, Mary will whip up a batch of home-made caramels for the neighborhood and then toss in a little ornament with each boxful. I do the same thing, somehow trying to find some magic formula that is a measure of how I feel about people. There are solutions, such as budgets, sticking with our first instinct, telling people how we feel about them, and ridding ourselves of guilt.

James Breig

Dueling dolls

One Christmas morning, just before dawn,
two toys for the children talked on and on;
One was a Cabbage Patch, dressed in a gown;
the other, a Rambo doll, wearing a frown.

"What a great morning," said Cabbie with glee;
"It's great to be sitting here under the tree;
just picture the faces of Janice and Bill."
Said Rambo: "I can't wait for the kill."

"That's awful," said Cabbie, "and horrible, too.
This morning is joyous for me and for you.
How can you talk about death and destruction
on the day that the world got a God-introduction?"

'Don't be so high-hat," responded the thug.
"We both will be played with; we'll both get a hug.
Kids like some mayhem with machine guns and tanks.
I'll bet my new owner gives Santa some thanks."

"It's sad," sniffed the other, awaiting adoption.
"I wish that that child had some brighter option
than playing with someone in camouflage gear."
And with that her eye shed a huge, pretend tear.

Rambo just snickered and loaded his gun.
"Me and that kiddie will have lots of fun.
Bang goes a village; boom goes a town;
I cannot wait for that kid to come down."

Cabbage Patch shuddered and started to speak,
but then on the stairs she heard a small squeak

Finding God in Your House

as children crept down to peer under the tree
and scoop up their presents with ''Yow'' and ''Yippee!''

So Cabbage Patch closed her eyes with a wish
as a hand picked her up and hugged her a squish
while someone else rat-a-tatted a gun
and mounted the body count past one hundred and one.

She opened her eyes to see her child's thrill
and discovered the hugger was none other than Bill,
while Janice and Rambo slaughtered people galore
and waded about in bodies and gore.

The moral is simple and easy to phrase:
Choose presents wisely when buying these days;
and if you want to liberate brother,
make sure that you don't imprison the other.

Have yourself a hectic little Christmas

This Christmas, if it's all the same to you, I'd prefer that you
fill my living room with pipers piping, swans swimming and
geese ovulating. All these fowl and musicians would be down-
right soothing compared to what happened to my family during twelve hectic days of Christmas last year when we had missing teeth and coats, and a surprise in our washing machine.

I want to tell readers what happened because next to this ar-
ray of misfortune your Christmas will look positively placid;
and you'll enjoy your holidays, regardless of how filled they
are with shopping, decorating and partying.

On the other hand, when I think of the wacky goings-on, I
could even argue in favor of your experiencing what we did
because, despite what happened, last Christmas was one of the

159

most pleasant holidays I can remember. Let me consider that paradox while I tell you about The Attack of the Goo, 48-degree temperatures indoors and The Case of the Telephoning Son.

It all began innocently a week before Christmas when my wife, Mary, and I attended her office party at a small restaurant-bar. It came with a live singer attached. He unpacked his guitar, said, ''How about some Elvis?'' and sang ''Blue Christmas,'' complete with amplifiers, from a distance of approximately three feet.

When we left, I held Mary's coat for her and she said, ''That's not mine, you idiot'' (she loves those cute terms of endearment). I replied, ''It better be yours because it's the only one on the rack.'' Someone had walked off with her coat and left us with one that was similar in color but two sizes larger and about a foot shorter.

We left our name, hoped that it was a misunderstanding born of liquid, and went home. Little did we suspect that the Coat Caper was just the beginning of several days of ever-increasing insanity.

The next morning delivered a daylong snowstorm that kept our three kids at home and plunked about eight wet, heavy inches of snow on us. I wondered why it didn't also bring down the power lines near us since the slightest weather disturbance (a cloud passing, for instance) seems to shut off electricity in our area. I didn't have long to wait to be anointed a prophet.

At 5 a.m. the next day, Matt, our 16-year-old, wandered into our bedroom to announce that the power had gone off at 3:30 a.m. We were delighted to know this at that hour, since it allowed us to lie wide-eyed in bed, waiting for dawn or electricity, whichever came first. Given the record of the power company

Finding God in Your House

in our area, we suspected who the winner would be. So, at 8, Mary and I went off to work powerless, which also meant heatless and hot-waterless.

Mary's coat surfaced (along, we presume, with the taker's sobriety). It was left to me to pick it up after work. Upon arrival at the restaurant, I was told by the employees that they didn't know what coat I was talking about. I mentioned a suit and they remembered the coat.

All day at work, I had assumed that the power would return; but every time I called home I was informed that the kids were still in the cold. So I advised my sons to bring in some firewood. When I got home with the coat, I built a roaring fire from the four logs they had managed to struggle in with. My sons approach wood work with the same speed as the pre-Dorothy Tin Woodman.

As the sun set on Friday, we all huddled in the living room. We used the fire for heat and candles for light; and we assumed that, any second, we would get electricity back. Old habits die hard, of course; so every time we would walk into the bathroom carrying a candle, we would automatically reach for the light switch. Of course, we made sure to turn it "off" when we left. Strangely, this did not affect the candles. Can science explain this phenomenon?

More firewood was needed before we slept, so I brought it to the back door; Mary ferried it to the living room. One load apparently strained her back, but we wouldn't know that for another day. Another ticking time bomb.

All night I snoozed like an Ice Age caveman, one eye closed and one on the fire to make sure it didn't go out. It's amazing how these primitive instincts return in such moments. (I was also concerned about relighting the fire. One of my sons claims I couldn't start a fire if I had a blowtorch and gasoline. Shows how much he knows. I bet I could. Two out of three times.)

The next day, Saturday, the power was still off. That was old news. Fresh news was that Mary couldn't stand without grunting. Another sign of the Ice Age? No; it was her back, showing the signs of strain from the firewood. So Mary went to the chiropractor's to have her back checked. This wouldn't ordinarily merit comment except for one fact: she works as a receptionist at the chiropractic office. That means free treatment; it also means wearing a hospital gown in front of fellow employees. But, in keeping with the season, she was now assuming the shape of a candy cane. So she swallowed her sense of privacy and went.

That night, for the second time, we all slept in the living room, like wagon-train passengers around the camp fire. The first night without light and heat was cozy, old-fashioned and romantic. The second was a pain in an area slightly below where Mary ached.

After $48^1/_2$ hours the electricity returned, and we stumbled sleepy-eyed to bed. This proved to be an error on Mary's part; the next morning, she couldn't get out of bed because her back hurt. This Sunday morning was the dawn of our wedding anniversary. Happy anniversary, Mary; I'd kiss you, but I can't get low enough to reach your lips. She spent the rest of her day on the couch. Alone.

During her convalescence, Mary couldn't go to work. She had started work there in October and got five sick days. She had now used $3^1/_2$ of them nursing a sore back. Not exactly great advertising for the boss. Each of those days, she visited one of the three chiropractors who staff her office. I finally wondered, "Is there anyone at your office now who hasn't seen you naked?" She named the cleaning lady.

On Christmas Eve, Mary and I decided to challenge the gods of oddity who had been plaguing us by exchanging our anniversary presents, which had lain in their wrappings untouched. Maybe this would change our luck, we thought. Mary gave me a videotape of "White Christmas," which we saw on our honeymoon. I gave her . . . a videotape of "White Christmas," which we saw on our honeymoon. Happy anniversary, dear.

By Christmas Mary had recovered enough to prepare a full turkey dinner. Trying to be a major help and win a Ms. magazine award, I decided to pitch in by throwing all the garbage—cole slaw leftovers, stuffing bits, corn—into the disposal. Only the disposal didn't dispose all. I'm about as handy around the house as the next guy, if the next guy is The Cat in the Hat, but I began to fiddle around anyway, to try to find the source of the problem. I tried the Broomstick Solution. Someone once told me to stick the handle in the disposal to dislodge any blockage. Fortunately he knew me well enough to explain also that the machine was supposed to be off when I did this or we would have splinters in our ceiling.

While I scratched my head, Mary found a new reason to worry. The garbage wasn't going down in the kitchen drain; it was coming up in the first-floor bathroom sink. Half of what I had shoved into the disposal now gurgled there.

The other half? It was discovered in the washing machine. Inside the tub, in place of socks and underwear, floated corn kernels and carrot shavings.

The plumber arrived next morning with his teenage son in

tow. I explained the problem as if I understood it and, handyman that I am, suggested that the cause lay in the disposal. The plumber smiled benignly (sort of the way adults smile when a 6-year-old explains his concept of how babies get made), went directly to the basement, and immediately located the pipe at fault. After I helped him move sleds, mattresses and old snow shovels, he said, "Good, you've got a floor drain." He opened the pipe and released black sewer water filled with cole slaw, corn, stuffing, turkey and some materials even Stephen King would gag at.

The floor drain turned out to be like the disposal and Mary's back: out of service. Now the floor was covered with a slimy goo. The phone rang; it was for the plumber. He listened for a while and made noncommittal sounds. Who was it? A mystery to be solved later. When he completed his chores and departed, Jimmy, our 17-year-old, and I began throwing newspapers on the mess to soak it up. The smell needed Lysol; we needed slaves.

Next I called Mary to tell her that the problem was sorta, kinda taken care of. She informed me that our across-the-street neighbor had phoned her at work to complain that the plumber's son had tossed a snowball at her dog, an offense she ranked between kidnapping and selling arms to Iran. Mary suggested to her that we are not responsible for the plumber's son and recommended that the neighbor call the plumber. First mystery solved: that was the call he got.

The next mystery was The Case of the Telephoning Son. It began when Matthew phoned, asking to be picked up at the shopping center. You got there by bus, I informed him; return the same way. After he plea-bargained, a compromise was reached:

Finding God in Your House

he'd take a bus to downtown, and I'd get him there. He agreed to call me when he reached downtown.

Meanwhile I set about preparing lunch for Mary, who didn't want to come home and risk injuring her back by helping Jimmy and me clean the basement. (I bought this excuse, by the way, a sign of how wacky I was becoming.) Since she had the car that I needed to retrieve Matt, Jimmy drove me to her work so I could pick up the car. I delivered the lunch, and Mary informed me that she didn't like wholewheat bread. I considered telling her another way to consume it, which would bypass her taste buds. I resisted on the basis I wouldn't get free treatments for spine injuries incurred from well-placed kicks. Instead, I said, "I'm taking the car to get Matt."

In the five minutes Jimmy and I were at her office, what we didn't want to happen happened. Matt called home and got no answer. So he phoned his mom, naturally reaching her just after I left. She informed him that "Dad's on his way," interpreting my comment about the car as "I'm going NOW to pick him up" when I meant "I've got to get him SOMETIME today."

Jimmy and I returned home to await Matt's call (which had already come, only I didn't know it). To kill time, I sent Jimmy to the store and helped him to his car with soda-bottle empties. In the two minutes I was outside, guess who called? Right—Matthew. But there should have been no problem since Carrie, our 8-year-old, was now home from visiting a friend. She answered.

"Where's Dad?" Matt asked. "I don't know," she replied, putting the phone down and going back to playing with Christie.

I came back inside to await the call that had come twice. Only I still didn't know it.

165

James Breig

With all this going on, I decided it was time for a treat. Something to help me forget the craziness surrounding me. Ah, a box of caramels, which Mary had given me for Christmas. Approximately 1.7 seconds after the candy entered my mouth, I knew what was about to happen. It happened at 1.9 seconds. I took the half-chewed chocolate from my mouth and it now had, in place of a caramel center, a "crown" center. The sticky thing had pulled out not only the fake tooth, but also the post that held it in place.

I now had a gaping hole in my mouth, soaked newspapers on the basement floor, a crippled wife, a missing song, and two copies of "White Christmas."

I picked up the phone to call the dentist and heard the "beep-beep-beep" chorus from the opera "Off-the-hook." A search turned up the source of the noise: the mouthpiece of the phone in our bedroom resting on the table. I quizzed Carrie. "Oh, yeah, Matt called." "What did he want?" "You." But why? To be picked up? To change the location? To say he got a ride?

She shrugged.

I called Mary to share my latest predicament. "Matt called here an hour ago," she informed me. I looked for a gas pipe. Hah! If we had gas, we would have had hot water a week before. So I did something more dangerous: called the dentist. His answering service informed me that he wouldn't be in until Tuesday. This was Friday. I left my name and Mary's phone number and asked that he call. Surely he would take pity on me in my emergency state.

When we got back, I called Mary to ask if she'd heard from the dentist yet. "I'm talking to him now," she said. "I'll have him call you."

Finding God in Your House

He did. "Hurt?" he asked. Nope. "See you Tuesday," he said.

That's when I began longing for pipers piping, maids milking, or drummers drumming.

And that's how my Christmas went. I'm glad it's gone. But, oddest of all, it wasn't that horrible a holiday. As I told friends who listened openmouthed to these tales. "It was nothing major. Just a series of minor annoyances."

I don't wish such a Christmas on you, but I wouldn't mind if you experienced the same sort of slowed-down pace that allowed us to laugh over duplicate gifts, to wonder together when it would all end, and to have a great story to tell for Christmases to come.

On the other hand, there was my dentist's heartchilling sentence as I finally sat in his chair to have the crown replaced: "I'll have to trim your gums."

The words "trim" and "gums" should never appear in proximity to each other. To avoid that again, I'll take the French hens and even the lords a-leaping.

CHAPTER 11

The Ten Commandments come home

Do you worship one God?

Let's talk about the Ten Commandments and what they mean to modern families. Take the first commandment: "I, the Lord, am your God. You shall not have other gods besides me."

Sounds ridiculous, right? How many families are worshiping Thor or Zeus or Baal? After all, worshiping means giving your entire self to someone or something. Webster defines worship as "extreme devotion; intense love or veneration." And families don't build altars to Athena, light candles to Wodan or bow down before graven images.

But some families do have other "gods." Here are some questions for all of us to ask ourselves around the dinner table to test how well we live up to the First Commandment:

• How many times this year have we skipped Sunday Mass? What did we substitute in its place—a vacation? sleep? a ball game?

• How often do we pray in a given week? Compare that number with how many TV shows we watch in one day.

• Name the last five books we have read. How many of them are about God, Jesus, the church, prayer or some other part of our faith?

• Whose pictures are displayed in our home?

Finding God in Your House

- How many bank accounts do we have? How often do we worry about money? How much time do we spend every day reading about investments? How frequently do we complain about our income, about taxes, about bills? How much does money occupy our minds? For comparison, how often does God enter our thinking?

- A question for children about the future: do you want to grow up to be like Jesus? Or do you copy rock stars, sports figures, TV actors and others?

Conclude your discussion with a prayer:

"Lord, our only God, fix in our hearts a singular love for you. Keep our minds—easily distracted by everyday worries, the lure of money and other small gods—focused on the one God who has saved us, the one God who can bring us peace, the one God who has given us all we need for eternal happiness. Amen."

Don't swear your life away

The Second Commandment is the one most of us break when we stub our toes: "You shall not take the Lord's name in vain."

The Second Commandment seems like an easy one to apply to our lives. Listen to any movie and you'll hear characters mentioning God's power to damn. Likewise, many of us have fallen into the habit of using the phrase "Jesus Christ" not as a prayer but in place of the much simpler "ouch." (That reminds me of the witticism uttered by G.K. Chesterton, who said—I'm paraphrasing—that people can be led to state great theological truths they don't believe in simply by shutting a door on their fingers.)

169

James Breig

So we can obey the Second Commandment by cleaning our mouths out with soap, right? Wrong. But it's a good first step. If we're going to get into the habit of using foul words, we'd be better off choosing ones that don't lower God's name.

But obeying the Second Commandment means more than the negative message of having us stop doing something. It also means something positive: having us put more meaning into our prayers so that, when we do say the words "God" and "Jesus Christ," they have some significance. It also means being able to utter those names in public without embarrassment. Too many Christians flinch when they say "Jesus Christ," as if he were a criminal cousin they would rather not talk about. If we are to follow his command to spread his message throughout the world, a good first step would be learning to pronounce his name with pride.

Businesses hire lawyers and public-relations firms and they spend millions of dollars every year to keep their "good name." They'll sue if their copyright is infringed; they'll go to court if another company uses a similar name; they get upset if their name becomes attached to something negative. (Think of the consternation that must have been felt by the makers of those diet products that have the same name as AIDS.)

Each of us has a similar feeling about our own name, especially our family name. More and more women are keeping their maiden names after marriage; we make sure people can spell our names correctly; we take time to teach people how to pronounce our names, something I've battled for decades. If someone tried to make our name a swear word, I bet we'd do something drastic.

Yet many of us don't have the same attitude toward God's

name. We should make it something sacred, something we pronounce with familiarity but also with awe, something we utter with respect and honor.

Keeping the Second Commandment means scrubbing our mouths, but it also means restoring luster to God's name. Most of all, it means improving our prayer lives so that speaking God's name becomes something we do often and with vigor.

I wish it were Sunday; that's my fun day

What do you do on Sunday?

Sleep late? Watch the big game on the tube? Sprawl on the couch and take a leisurely journey through the newspaper? Head for the mall to stroll among the shoppers?

The Third Commandment—"Remember to keep holy the Lord's Day"—is an easy one to apply to our lives, but it also raises some of the stickiest issues because it is so close to home:

• Do you go to church as a family? Or does everyone have his or her own favorite Mass based on its time, location, celebrant and other factors?

• How many of the 52 weekends of the year find you in church at all? As a family unit?

• What excuses do you use to skip Mass (body temperature above 99, outside temperature below 32, traveling, "We went twice in a row this month," fatigue from the party the night before) and how legitimate are they?

Keeping holy the Lord's day means more than showing up in church on Sunday or Saturday evening. It also means making the Sabbath into something more than one-seventh of the week. The workday world often prevents us from exploring

171

our faith, from reading about religion, from praying, from teaching our children about God, from volunteering to help others, and from doing many other things that fall under the heading of "holiness."

An hour at Mass on Sunday morning followed by three to six hours with football players is slightly out of whack. John Madden won't make you holier. Here are some ideas for keeping the Lord's day a little holier; check the ones you plan to do:

( ) After Mass I will spend another hour reading a book about religion.

( ) On one Sunday a month, I will volunteer in a parish program.

( ) Between now and the Super Bowl, I will give up the time needed to watch one televised football game. Instead, I will do something for someone I love.

( ) I will pray for fifteen minutes before reading the Sunday paper.

( ) To make Sundays holier, I will (fill in your own idea):

Mom and Dad, where would I be without you?

Moms and dads have eagerly awaited our arrival at commandment number four: "Honor your father and your mother." I can imagine all of you telling the kids to sit down and give a listen, cuz this one's for them.

But, surprise, it's also for you. Paulist Father Richard Sparks, assistant professor of Christian ethics at the College of St. Thomas in St. Paul, Minnesota, explains that the Fourth Com-

Finding God in Your House

mandment "originally was understood to mean, 'Don't turn your back on persons who gave you life itself.' Today, you could tie it in with how we treat the elderly, nursing homes, Social Security. Not caring for the elderly could be a way of turning our back. Justice requires care in general'' for the mothers and fathers of the world.

A belief in extending "mothers and fathers" to mean the world's enlarging population of aged folks was supported by Sue Carter, a social worker in the aging program of Catholic Charities in the Archdiocese of St. Paul-Minneapolis. "Honor and communicate with your elders," she says, interpreting the commandment for modern people, "for they may have the wisdom to share from their experiences in life."

Ralph Martin, writing in *Pastoral Renewal* newsletter, extends the Fourth Commandment even further: "The most dangerous attacks against this commandment are not usually frontal. People who blatantly advocate . . . rejecting parents are few, and their arguments do not win over many people. Much more dangerous is the prevailing cultural ethos, which casts suspicion on every form of personal authority (including that of parents) and promotes individual freedom (including that of children) at the expense of social responsibility."

So keeping the Fourth Commandment includes:

• Revering, respecting and honoring your own parents no matter their age or yours.

• Caring for society's elderly population in general.

• Recognizing and respecting the wisdom that comes with years and allowing that wisdom to be heard and heeded.

• Coming to a philosophy of how your individual freedom fits into the good of society at large.

Doing those things means more than obeying Dad's order to shovel the sidewalk or mow the lawn. It might mean taking Dad in when Alzheimer's strikes, voting for increased Medicare payments, ridding ourselves of the notion that "young is good, old is bad," bringing our children up in a way that encourages them to respect us and gives them reasons to, submitting our personal wishes to the commonweal.

(Thanks to the *Catholic Bulletin,* newspaper of the St. Paul-Minneapolis archdiocese, for the Minnesota information.)

Killing me softly

When I was a young boy, obeying the Fifth Commandment, "Thou shalt not kill," was easy. Since I didn't possess any weapons and rarely felt the urge to do more to my little sister than ignore her, the Fifth Commandment didn't often show up during Confession.

Then I began to grow and to reflect on the commandment. At the same time, society was changing. Killing, previously the sole province of skulking murderers and insane tyrants, was becoming society's business as abortion and euthanasia became more and more commonplace. As for me, I was starting to recognize in myself the killer in another sense: the angry man, the vengeful human, the screaming father, the verbally abusive husband.

Yes, the Fifth Commandment, which at one time seemed to be violated only by Mansons and Hitlers, suddenly had new applications in my life and in the world. Just ask yourself some of these questions:

• What about racism and sexism? Can Christians kill another's spirit by their attitudes?

174

Finding God in Your House

• What about our failure as citizens to vote for peace around the world? How responsible are we for turning children in Ireland and Israel and Iran into machine-gun-toting terrorists?

• What about world hunger? How many people do we kill by our overconsumption of leisure and recreation while they starve?

• What about the death penalty, infanticide, mercy killing?

• Are we Americans killing our environment—including many living creatures and maybe including ourselves—with pollution?

Those are huge questions to ask ourselves as we examine our consciences. But we must also ask questions that bring us closer to home and closer to our hearts: are we verbally or physically abusive to our families or employees? Do we fill our minds with violent images through television, movies and books? How quickly do we become angry in shopping lines or waiting rooms or traffic jams?

Filling our lives with life takes effort when we are surrounded by death. Not participating in that death-making requires a commitment to God and to his son's instructions on how to live: as a servant, sacrificially, humbly, like a child.

Honey, I'll never be untrue

In this article about sex, I admit "committing adultery."

A statement such as that guarantees attention. Getting the word "sex" into the sentence and promising a *National Enquirer-*style confession means that this is one article you won't skip.

"Sex" gets attention because we live in a country that is fascinated by sex. Fascinated? How about obsessed with sex?

For proof, switch on the TV and see what sells most products advertised. Or take a drive and look at the billboards. Or check the contents of the morning newspaper. Everywhere you look, sex can be found. And be honest: every day you live, you think about sex in some form. There's nothing wrong with that. After all, God invented sex, intended us to use it wisely, and made it something appealing and pleasurable.

It wasn't God who turned sex into Joan Collins, *Penthouse*, incest and child porn. And if we can excuse ourselves from that extreme list, let's remember that God also didn't turn sex into X-rated videotapes on the home VCR, dirty jokes around the water cooler, the labeling of all women as sex objects and Dr. Ruth.

By now, you've probably figured out that I'm talking about the Sixth Commandment: "You shall not commit adultery."

As for my committing adultery, I have to admit I tricked you a little. But most men my age have committed adultery several times—when we were 12. Those adulteries all occurred in grade school, when boyhood confessions frequently included numerous violations of the Sixth Commandment. Boys in those days often owned up to "bad thoughts" about girls and such thoughts (along with peeks at *Playboy*) were considered acts of adultery.

We joke now about that notion, but was it really so far off? After all, didn't Jesus teach us about sinning in our hearts; and doesn't society today demand that we not look at women as sex objects? Maybe we boys of the '50s were on the right track and were 30 years ahead of everyone else in realizing that we were responsible for our thoughts.

In that light, maybe married couples today need to look again at the Sixth Commandment. It forbids adultery, but there are

Finding God in Your House

ways to violate it without cheating on your spouse. Examine your conscience by using these questions:

( ) Do I treat my spouse as someone to give me pleasure rather than as someone to love in a mutual, sharing way?

( ) What image of sex do I present to my children—a healthy one in which sex is part of life, a gift from God, and something to be treated with care and respect? Or is the image a warped one in which sex is something to be snickered at, joked about and made into a locker-room topic?

( ) How well have I educated myself and my children about sex? Does that education include moral instruction as well as biological information?

( ) Do I consider any of the following to be sinful: reading *Playboy*? watching R-rated movies? renting X-rated videos? Telling dirty jokes? Fantasizing about someone other than my spouse?

( ) Would I apply the word "sacred" to my marriage? To the sexual relationship I have with my spouse?

( ) How much thought, study and reading have I given to what God intends sexuality to be? Contrast that to the thought, study and reading I've given to how society defines sexuality. Is the balance out of whack?

( ) How often have I made sexual intercourse into something it should not be, such as a burden, a duty or a demand?

( ) In what ways can I adjust my marriage to be more in line with what God intends it to be?

( ) Do I overemphasize sex as a sin, especially in other people's lives?

The Sixth Commandment asks a lot of modern people because of where we live and the age we live in.

Here's an idea you can steal

One thousand high-school students were asked recently in a Gallup poll to name the Ten Commandments. It turned out that the Seventh Commandment was the easiest for them to remember.

There was no explanation why "thou shall not steal" stood out from the remainder. Perhaps it is popular because it is so simple (no odd language about "false witness" and "neighbor's wife") and one that children realize they are capable of violating (unlike "thou shall not kill"). Perhaps it was popular because we all recognize the many ways in which we can steal. It doesn't take a bank robber to sin against the Seventh Commandment.

We take what is not rightfully ours in many different ways. Here is a list of how we steal, what we steal and who we steal from:

How we steal	What we steal	Who we steal from
Loafing at work	Time	Our employer, fellow workers
Abusing the environment	Natural beauty	God, everyone
Ignoring our families	Love, attention	Loved ones

Finding God in Your House

How we steal	What we steal	Who we steal from
Being apathetic about politics	Better society	Fellow citizens
Being prejudiced	Equality	Everyone
Cheating on income taxes	Money	Government, other taxpayers, the poor

Talk together about what stealing is. Expand on the list by providing examples from your experience and imagination.

And feel free to borrow any of the above.

Honest to God

Truth to tell, in our continuing series of reflections on the Ten Commandments, we've reached number eight: "You shall not bear dishonest witness against your neighbor." Honest, we've gone through the other seven. Believe me, it's gone fast. It truly seems like we just began this series. Really, it does.

Truth to tell . . . honest . . . believe me . . . truly . . . really. Those are words and phrases we constantly sprinkle throughout our conversations to convince others that we are being truthful and upfront. Some psychologists will tell you to beware when people overuse such expressions; they are often compensations behind which lurk lies, distortions, overuse and misrepresentations—like the unethical salesperson who grins and asks, "Would I cheat you?"

The media today are a lot like that salesperson. They cloak gossip, rumor, and slander behind high-sounding terms such as "reality TV," "documentary examinations," and "inside info." As for government, it seems that our age is not only a time of outright lying but also of distortion, cover-up and truth

179

twisting. And what about big business? Insider trading, shoddy goods, the dumping of inferior products on poor nations, excessive profits—all of those can be violations of the Eighth Commandment.

And that's our article about the commandment against lying.

Except for one group: us. It would be dishonest if we didn't also look at ourselves in relation to the Lord's command against lying. After all, the temptations to lie confront us every day:

• When the boss asks us who fouled up the project ("He did; I had nothing to do with it.");

• When our spouse wonders what we're thinking ("Nothing much.");

• When the kids ask us if we have time to help them with their homework ("Not now, later.");

• When a phone caller asks for a donation to a charity ("I gave at the office.");

• When we feel prompted by God to do something that would inconvenience us ("I'll think about that tomorrow.");

• When we come to the moment at Mass when we think about our sins during the past week ("I'm okay.").

We kid ourselves; we pass the buck; we hide from the truth; we duck responsibility; we take the easy way out; we look at the media, government and business and say, "If I were in charge, it would be different." In short, we find all kinds of ways to lie. To ourselves, to our families and friends, to God.

Lying isn't just looking someone in the eye and saying something that isn't true. Lying is more devious than that. Lying, after all, is based on a lie.

Finding God in Your House

You mean I don't have to fall in love with my next-door neighbor?

The Ten Commandments prove one thing: Jews of Moses' time were just as hung up on sex as Americans of the late twentieth century. After all, 20 percent of the commandments concern sex. There's the Sixth Commandment against adultery and the Ninth Commandment, which says, "You shall not covet your neighbor's wife."

We might be tempted to turn feminist and say, "The Ninth Commandment is nowadays a plea for men to stop treating women as objects to be passed back and forth like borrowed lawn mowers."

But I'd like to rewrite the commandment to include women as violators, not just as victims. Let's make the commandment read like this: "You shall not treat your marriage as anything less than a sacred covenant." By doing that, we equalize the commandment so that it applies to both husbands and wives. When we do that, we see how applicable it is to modern times.

Our age does not respect marriage. Divorce, cheating, spouse abuse, abandonment—those are just some of the ways husbands and wives fail to live up to the Ninth Commandment. When we fall short of making marriage a sacred intertwining of two equal people, we don't keep this commandment.

We violate the Ninth Commandment when we:
- force our spouse into a subservient role;
- envy our neighbor's marriage without working to make ours better;

- fail to recognize trouble signs in our marriage and fail to take steps to correct them;
- put our marriage way down on our priority list—below career and financial security, for instance—of things to accomplish to have a "happy life";
- fail to give public witness to the importance of marriage.

Why is it always greener on the other side?

We have arrived at the Tenth Commandment: "You shall not desire your neighbor's house or field, nor his male or female slave, nor his ox or ass, nor anything that belongs to him."

Pretty easy to keep, right? My neighbors, as far as I can tell, don't own slaves or livestock and their field consists of a backyard just large enough to hold two pieces of lawn furniture.

But then we come to that catch-all phrase that God was smart enough to include: you shall not covet anything that belongs to your neighbor. And "anything" includes her job, his lawn, her car, his talent, their children, her charm, his relationship with his parents, her promotion, their kids' clothes. . . .

Well, you get the idea. As one Catholic rewrote it, the last commandment says this: "Be satisfied with what you have, and be happy when others succeed."

That advice goes against the way of life of many Americans, who base their existence on keeping up with the Joneses, surpassing their co-workers, getting ahead of the car in front of them and consuming voraciously. As one wit put it, "It isn't enough to succeed; our best friends must also fail."

So, okay, I decide to be content with what I've got and to

Finding God in Your House

be happy that the family down the block has a bigger patio and a faster car. I've fulfilled the commandment, right?

Well, not quite. Because more and more Catholics are coming to understand that this commandment also involves reaching out to other neighbors—the ones who might be tempted to covet what we have. If we live in such a way as to suppress those below us, then we are violating the spirit of the Tenth Commandment. And if you need some help in understanding that, both the Pope and the American bishops have written documents on the economy that give guidelines on how we are to relate to the needy.

So the last commandment, far from being an easy one to keep as long as the people next door don't own slaves, turns out to be very complex. This commandment means:

1. We have to stop envying others.

2. We have to appreciate who we are and what we have.

3. We have to work for those in need.

4. We have to understand that our "neighbors" include everyone in the world. (Remember Jesus' story about the Good Samaritan?)

5. To accomplish the first four on this list, we need to live the other nine commandments.

With an assignment like that, aren't you glad there isn't an Eleventh Commandment? God only knows what that might have demanded of us.

CHAPTER 12

Mercy works at home

Have you ever tried to counsel the doubtful?

A lot of baby-boomers spent a lot of time making fun of the "old church" in the wake of the Second Vatican Council. Jokes were told about scary confessionals, nuns with hand-whacking rulers, buying pagan babies, toting up indulgences, and other old-fashioned practices. I don't hear as many jokes as I used to, though. More and more, it seems, Catholics in their 30s and 40s are starting to recognize the value in some of those old ways and to reclaim the best of them.

For instance, it was considered smart for a while to ridicule the lists of virtues, vices, fruits of the Holy Spirit and other categories that had grown up in the pre-Council years. Lately, however, people are beginning to recognize the value in categorizing things, not as magical lists guaranteeing heaven but as systems of measuring our spiritual growth.

Let's go through one of those lists—the seven spiritual works of mercy—to see how it applies to modern Catholic families. According to one source, the spiritual works of mercy are "works of spiritual assistance—motivated by love of God and neighbor—to persons in need." Can you name the seven? Dig back in your memory banks and see how many of them you can recall:

Finding God in Your House

1. Counseling the doubtful.
2. Instructing the ignorant.
3. Admonishing sinners.
4. Comforting the afflicted.
5. Forgiving offenses.
6. Bearing wrongs patiently.
7. Praying for the living and the dead.

Let's start with counseling the doubtful. It seems like a daunting task, especially when each of us has our own doubts, hesitations and confusions about certain parts of our faith or spiritual life. We might be puzzled by this or that scripture passage or upset by some church regulation, but some people are doubting on a more basic level. They are struggling with belief in God or acceptance of the power of prayer or understanding God's love for them. Those people could be in our own families or among our friends, neighbors or co-workers. I know an adult woman with an alcoholic father who wonders if God could really care about her. I know teenagers who see no value in praying because God has more important people to worry about. I know a man who considers religion as the last remnant of medieval sorcery.

You can probably draw up your own list of doubters. Do you feel capable of counseling them? You don't have to have a degree to do so; counseling, in this case, could mean:

- Praying for them.
- Living your faith as an example for them to follow.
- Answering their questions about your beliefs and feelings.
- Listening to them nonjudgmentally when they want to express their feelings.
- Offering them reading material about their questions.

185

- Directing them to programs or persons that deal with their doubts.

Look around you. If you see someone doubting, offer him or her help in a gentle, inviting way.

Hey, stupid, wanna know about Jesus?

I don't recommend beginning a conversation with the title of this piece. But that may be your temptation when you're confronted with a desire to live out the second spiritual work of mercy: instruct the ignorant.

Applying "instruct the ignorant" should begin with understanding that the ignorant are not the stupid. "Ignorant" means "lacking knowledge," not "lacking the ability to know." All of us are ignorant about something. If you don't agree, I await your explanation of nuclear physics, the art of the Aztecs, the biology of slugs and Venusian mineralogy.

To a certain extent, all Christians are ignorant about God. After all, God is unknowable. If we could know God completely, we would be God. But some of us know more than others about God, religion, prayer, the Bible and other parts of faith. When we share that information with others, we are instructing the ignorant. The ignorant, in this instance, includes:

- Our children, whom we teach through our example as well as through reading to them, praying with them and leading them in the right direction;

- The unchurched, those without any formal religion, whom we teach through our example, by supporting missionaries and evangelists and by praying;

- Each other, whom we enlighten by sharing our experiences,

feelings, understandings and insights while they do the same with us.

- Ourselves, whom we inform by asking God for help in understanding what we fail to comprehend. Once we were blind about various parts of belief, but now we see. When we do, we can pass that (in)sight on to others.

Example turns up again and again in the above list. That's because example is a great teacher. That's how the cliché goes, and it's accurate. We Christians teach the loudest when we live what we believe. In that way, we instruct constantly and convincingly.

Love that sinner; hate that sin

Have you ever sidled up to someone and informed her about her specific vices? When was the last time you phoned a friend to tell him that he had better stop sinning? How often do you speak to your spouse about his or her moral failures?

At first thought, you might think that "never" is the correct answer to all those questions. But let's talk a while about it; maybe we're practicing this specific spiritual work of mercy more often than we admit. This spiritual work of mercy is, of course, "admonishing sinners."

At first glance, admonishing sinners might not seem like something we're likely to do ever, much less make a common part of our Christian activity. After all, we live in a society that treasures privacy. Popular slogans tell us to mind our own business, to stay out of other people's lives, not to meddle.

But Christians know that humans live in communities and are related to one another. We are not islands; we are archipelagos.

James Breig

What we do sends out echoes and ripples that have consequences beyond ourselves. The better we can make ourselves, the better the community; and the better the community, the better we are. So we work on both sides of the equation: bettering ourselves and bettering the community, and the latter means we sometimes have to admonish sinners.

That does not mean we publicly berate people we think are evil. "Admonish" means to "warn, cautiously advise, to exhort, to reprove with mildness." Admonishing is not a bright red stop sign with a state trooper in the bushes; it's a yellow flashing light at an intersection. In the New Testament, the early Christians gave examples of how to admonish: not by sewing scarlet letters on people, but by taking them aside and talking with them in private.

Now go back to the questions at the start of this article. Would you still say "never" to them? Think again; I'll bet you've done some of the following:

• Spoken calmly to a child about his temper tantrums and the problems he is having at school as a result;

• Talked to your teenager about her tendency to ignore her friends except when she needs them and about the danger of losing them because of that;

• Put your arm around your spouse while suggesting he or she has started putting work above the home on the priority list;

• Given advice on the phone to a friend about his drinking and offered to be there when he's tempted;

• Listened openly while your sister explained her problems and then gently advised her that she is the cause of some of them.

We've all done things like those; we've certainly all been in

188

the position of having the chance to do them. Maybe we didn't see them as exercises in a spiritual work of mercy, but that's what they were. When we did them, we were not hypocrites saying we don't have faults; we were not "holier-than-thou" Christians pretending we don't sin. We were simply offering what expertise or experience we have. That can derive from our lack of a certain sin or from our committing that sin and our subsequent ability to overcome it. When we admonish, we are often saying, "I've been down that road, and it's a dead end."

Finally, we have to remember the flip side of this spiritual work of mercy: we are sometimes on the receiving end. We might be the sinner someone else has to admonish. When that happens, we should recognize the effort they are making to warn us and slow down to see what they're warning us about.

How you can be a bottle of Bactine

When was the last time you kissed a child's boo-boo? Have you ever listened to a friend as she complained about her job? When your spouse has had a rough day at work, do you rub his back, buy her favorite ice cream, suggest a movie out together? Do you have a reputation for being someone who can be counted on when things go wrong?

If you answered yes to any of the above, congratulations! You've been practicing a spiritual work of mercy. The work of mercy we practice by kissing cuts, offering a listening ear, rubbing backs or bringing home peach swirl is "comforting the afflicted."

James Breig

Sometimes we think we have to volunteer our summers in Ethiopia working among the starving to be living examples of one who comforts the afflicted. But when most of us think of the works of mercy that way, we are setting impossible goals and setting ourselves up to feel guilty because we're not Albert Schweitzer, Mother Teresa or a super-combo of both. But, when you think about it, neither was Jesus. I mean, when he comforted the afflicted, he didn't take off for India or Africa; he went down the street in his hometown and started comforting. He cured the deaf guy on the corner; he soothed his friend's relatives when they mourned; he leaned back and listened to the woman at the well. In other words, he kissed boo-boos, rubbed backs and offered a friendly ear.

The afflicted are all around us (pssst: they are even, sometimes, us). The afflicted include:

• Our children when puberty turns out to be rougher than they thought and not just because of zits;

• Our spouses when the wild dreams of 25-year-olds turn into the humdrum realities of 40-year-olds;

• Our parents when the empty nest is lonelier than they imagined;

• Our friends when a job is lost, a child rebels or a calamity hits.

We become works-of-mercy practitioners when we set aside our comfort or our own woes and worries to help such people. You probably do some of that already. Why not give yourself credit for what you've done and then make an effort to do more? I'll bet that in the next seven days someone is going to come to you for comfort. You'll be tempted to respond with accusations or by ignoring them or by half-listening. Instead, think of this article and try to offer genuine comfort.

I'll say it: "I'm sorry"

Love Story, the popular 1970s novel by Erich Segal and the equally successful film, contributed a one-liner to America: "Love means never having to say you're sorry."

Guess what. He got it exactly backward. If the Gospels mean something more to us than Segal's work (and they do, in the same proportion that the sun is brighter than a penlight), Christians believe that love is always saying you're sorry. Love includes asking for, receiving and handing out forgiveness. Love means being able to say, "I'm sorry," and its sometimes more difficult cousin: "That's okay; forget it." The latter can be more difficult to get out because we love to hang on to grudges. Asking for forgiveness is difficult, but there's obviously something in it for us: peace of mind. So we learn to say, "I'm sorry" and "Please forgive me." But doling out forgiveness is another matter; doing that means we have to give up such goodies as having control over someone else, making someone feel guilty, nurturing anger and resentment, and cuddling revenge close to us. So we don't easily say, "Aw, forget it; I have" or "No problem."

But forgiving offenses is a spiritual work of mercy, something Christians should cultivate. Previous examples have been a little more palatable because they have involved our doing something for another person, such as counseling them or instructing them or comforting them. We didn't have to do anything risky as far as our inner feelings were concerned. But

191

James Breig

this one—forgiving offenses—means we have to do something very risky: we have to let go of revenge, we have to wave off being angry, we have to let someone off the hook at a time when we might enjoy letting them dangle a while longer.

When I think about this work of mercy in terms of families, I wonder if children do it more naturally than parents. Kids, it seems to me, are very adept at forgiving and forgetting and getting on to the next thing. Moms and dads, on the other hand, like to nail kids in the act ("Aha! Gotcha"), build up evidence against them ("Who else could have reached the cookie jar?"), call on witnesses ("Jamie says she didn't do it"), pass judgment ("You're lying"), and hand out the sentence ("You're grounded, mister"). A child's "I'm sorry" (frequently shown in a facial expression rather than in words) often brings a parental rebuke of "I doubt it" or "How's that going to fix the vase?"

Jesus was nailed to a cross by people who weren't apologetic; yet he still said, "Father, forgive them." Parents might want to practice a little of what Jesus preached and did.

If you skip this, I won't get mad

Turning the other cheek is one of Christ's most difficult teachings. The idea that, once punched, we should stand still for another sock is totally alien to most of us. We like heroes who fight back, preferably with nuclear capability. Imagine Arnold Schwarzenegger in a movie in which he is nailed to a cross. His enemies might get one hand secured, but Arnold would use the other to karate-chop his tormentors; then he'd grab the cross beam to batter his way to safety.

When his hand was nailed into the wood, Jesus put out the

Finding God in Your House

other. Turning the other cheek would be impossible to do—except that Jesus showed us it could be done. All through Holy Week, he bore wrongs patiently. One of his best friends ran away when he was arrested after being betrayed by another pal; he was forgotten by other followers, denied by Peter, reviled, spat on, whipped, scorned, lied about by false witnesses, and ultimately killed.

Bearing wrongs patiently is one of the spiritual works of mercy. We live in a society that sues when it smells even the faintest odor of mistreatment. I heard a news story the other day about a murder that resulted when two men argued over which of them had ordered a cheeseburger at a fast-food joint.

On a more personal and less grandiose scale, in our homes, we have all done the following:

• Given the silent treatment to a spouse who disappointed us;

• Sent children to their rooms for failing to eat the meal we slaved over;

• Slammed down the phone on annoying phone solicitors;

• Gossiped nastily about neighbors who shunned us;

• Cut off relatives who didn't give us all the attention we expected.

When we are wronged, we often react not with patience but with threats, anger, punishment and blame. Hanging on the cross, Jesus looked around and asked his father to forgive the people who were killing him. The next time someone annoys us, we might want to think about that.

I will never forget you

I have a batch of people I pray for every night as I lie in bed. Some of the names are constant; others on the list change as the needs of friends, relatives, co-workers and others shift. For instance, a friend contemplating a job change got on the list while he searched for new work and then dropped off when he found a position. But, a few months later when he was fired, he regained his prayer-list position.

Then there's my late brother-in-law Smitty. He was on my nightly list for a long time. He had cancer for several months. Smitty was not a religious man, but he was a good man who'd known a lot of troubles. He sometimes battled and won, sometimes fought and lost, sometimes battled back and struggled, but he always persevered. When his final trouble arrived, he asked me to start praying for him. As his days dwindled, he began planning his own funeral and reflecting on his life. Then one day, he got a letter.

Smitty had been married before and took his first wife's brother under his wing. The wife's mother had died, leaving the teenage boy adrift. Smitty took it upon himself to become the young man's guide and taught him the value of hard work and personal responsibility. Their lives separated after a few years; Smitty and his wife divorced, and time went on. Then the letter arrived. It was from the teenager, now a man in his early 60s. "You probably thought I forgot about you," the man wrote, "but I never did. You meant so much to me, and you straightened out my life. I love you."

Smitty told me that he was not afraid to die. With that teen on his conscience, it was no wonder.

Smitty, freed of pain and fatigue and worry, has time in eternity to pray for me. Praying for the living and the dead is a spiritual work of mercy, the last one of the seven we have been considering. It's probably the one most often practiced. At Mass

194

Finding God in Your House

we pray for the living and the dead; most of us have other times when we talk to God about loved ones. I have a weird habit of praying for strangers, people I read about in the paper and think might not have anyone else to pray for them. They get on my nighttime list along with Smitty and job-searching friends and my children and my wife.

The prayers that flow among Christians are part of an invisible network called the Mystical Body of Christ or the communion of saints. That network recognizes that we're all connected in some way we can't really fathom but which we nonetheless sense. Death doesn't sever the network because life still goes on in a different way.

AFTERWORD:

The second spring of Robin and Marian

They came back, like half-forgotten memories of gentle joy, to remind us that, sometimes, the simplest song is the prettiest music.

Three years ago, Robin and Marian came into our family in a very unusual way: They built a nest on top of a decorative pillar by our front door. Robin and Marian, of course, are robins. From our front window, we watched them find grass and twigs to construct their home; we saw Marian using her body to shape the formless mass into a bowl; we peeked at the three eggs she deposited there; we peeped at the triplets who were born a few weeks later: Doug, Larry and Admiral, cleverly named by me because they are birds (check your Baseball Encyclopedia for Doug Bird's identity).

Then they were gone. The trio had developed from helpless hatchlings to fully-licensed pilots who flew off to points unknown. Every spring, we looked for their return, but they never came back—until last spring. This time, they were trying to build a nest at our family room window where the brick sticks out a little. When they had failed on the pillar three years earlier, I had scrambled up a ladder and hammered a piece of drywall into place for their perch. Seeing the same difficulty last spring, I lugged the ladder to the window and clumsily nailed a piece of pine to the center of my window frame where the robins were

Finding God in Your House

stacking their nesting materials. They turned up their beaks at my offering and began building to the left but with the same level of success: none. The twigs and grass would not stay on the sloping brick. Back up I went; I tugged out the first set of nails and re-positioned the board to the left. Naturally, they went to the far right. Okay, I said, I'm not John James Audubon and I don't like rejection—and the expression "bird brain" is entirely accurate.

Left alone, the two diligent robins fought against the odds, which included the tiny space on the brick outcropping, its slope away from the house and the stupid guy with the ladder who kept ruining things with his hammer. Annoyed, I closed the curtains in the family room and wished them, sarcastically, good luck. Which is what they got. Somehow, their nest stuck to the brick, defied gravity and me, and soon cupped four tiny blue eggs.

Like three years before, we began peeping through the curtain at the progress of the Robin Family. We watched mom sitting on the eggs and remaining at her post even when she spotted our voyeurism; we counted the days to hatching as outlined by the World Book entry on robins; we exchanged nightly updates. Jimmy, our 20-year-old, became the protector of the birds, clucking at all of us that our peeking was disturbing the mother and delaying the hatching.

Nevertheless, as I announced one morning, "we achieved birds." Three of the eggs had burst into the ugliest group of guys and gals I've ever seen. The size of a little finger, they were pulsating masses of flesh with one or two half-formed feathers stuck haphazardly on their backs. Only a mother and father could love such creatures. And they did by keeping them

197

warm and feeding them and making noises at the Human Family who continued to eyeball the babies.

But what about the fourth egg? Laid later than the others, it didn't hatch with the rest. Would the contents be forgotten? a runt? ignored? left behind when the others flew off? We continued our sentry and up popped number four a few days later, smaller but feisty and ready to take his or her place among the rest of the family (the bird books don't explain how to distinguish genders in newborn robins).

Carrie, our 12-year-old, named the quadruplets Rhett, Scarlett, Melanie and Ashley. Her obsession with "Gone With The Wind" continues unabated. So did our daily checking of the babies as they began perking up, picking up their heads to demand food, peeping loudly when they were hungry and popping out in more acceptable plumage. As they grew bigger, they were crammed ever more tightly in the nest but they were reluctant to venture beyond its safe confines.

Then, one day, Melanie took the chance: She jumped the side of the nest and stood—where?—on the wood I had nailed up to the left! It had proved useful after all; it became a launching pad as each of the newborns flapped its wings in practice for the grand departure. Mom and dad sat nearby in the red maple tree, chirping encouragement at their offspring as each hip-hopped to the wood, flip-flopped his or her wings and leaped into the future.

One evening, arriving home from work, Mary and I checked the nest and found it empty. I waited a few more days to make sure no new tenants were coming. Then I laddered up again and yanked down my wooden platform. But I left the nest. We wonder if it will be another three years before they return. We

Finding God in Your House

wonder if the two adults were newcomers to our yard or if they were Robin and Marian come back to us like returning prodigals or if they were Doug or Larry or Admiral come back home with a wife to show off to the grandparents who had peeked out the window at them when they were just kids.

Whoever they were, they came at the right time. We needed them to remind us how much family closeness means to us, to re-teach us that the simplest things in life are the most important, and to underline once again that if God cares so much for the birds of the air he must be absolutely crazy-in-love with us.

When we're out on our nightly walks, Mary and I spot robins here and there and imagine that this one is the runt and that other is the brave one who first flapped out of our lives. Soon, they will be going south. The encyclopedia says that robins from our area sometimes winter in Georgia. That seems the perfect spot for Rhett, Scarlett, Melanie and Ashley.